BACKPACKER

Complete Guide to
Outdoor Gear Maintenance and Repair

Step-by-Step Techniques to Maximize Performance
and Save Money

Kristin Hostetter

FALCONGUIDES

GUILFORD, CONNECTICUT
HELENA, MONTANA
AN IMPRINT OF GLOBE PEQUOT PRESS

Copyright © 2012 Morris Book Publishing, LLC

Illustrations by Robert Prince; illustration on page 3 based on original art by Supercorn
Text design and layout: Nancy Freeborn
Project editor: Julie Marsh

Library of Congress Cataloging-in-Publication Data

Hostetter, Kristin.
Backpacker magazine's complete guide to outdoor gear maintenance and repair : step-by-step techniques to maximize performance and save money / Kristin Hostetter.
p. cm.
Includes index.
ISBN 978-0-7627-7831-7
1. Backpacking—Equipment and supplies. 2. Backpacking—Maintenance and repair. I. Title.
GV199.62.H67 2012
796.510284—dc23

2012008250

Printed in the United States of America
10 9 8 7 6 5 4 3

Contents

Preface

The way I see it, there are two types of hikers: those who love gear with a slightly bizarre passion (aka "gearheads") and those who barely even acknowledge its existence.

Gearheads call their backpacks by name, they get a little weepy-eyed talking about their boots, and they've sewn up their favorite jacket so many times that it looks like a patchwork quilt. They also swoon over the latest and greatest gear; even if they don't buy it, they love learning about it.

For those folks in the other camp—the ones who are nonchalant, maybe even a bit cavalier about their gear—it's simply the means to the end. They just gather up their stuff and hit the trail. They don't covet shiny new gizmos, fawn over the latest technologies, or give it much thought at all . . . until something goes wrong.

Whether you fall into one of these extreme camps or somewhere in the middle, this book is aimed at you. Your outdoor experience will be a lot more comfortable—and fun—if you know how to "MacGyver" your way out of a sticky situation. Plus, you'll save boatloads of money and lessen your environmental impact if you keep your gear in good repair, rather than ditch it and buy something new when a problem strikes.

For this book I wanted to really get my hands dirty. During my fifteen-plus years as BACK-PACKER magazine's gear editor, I've written about gear repairs more times than I can remember. It's funny how repairs look so easy when you read about them and look at the nice clean line drawings that show you the steps. The reality of gear repair is far grimier, which is why I solicited real gear from real people for this book. I wanted

to make all the repairs myself and shoot photos in the process. So I launched a campaign on Facebook and backpacker.com, asking readers to send me their busted-up, worn-out gear to work on. And they did, by the box load! I learned a lot during this process, and it made me feel great to be able to lend a hand to my fellow hikers.

This book is cram packed with not only all the repairs and fix-it tips I've learned along the way, but also a ton of general gearhead advice:

- **Tips from the Field:** These sections include ideas for keeping your gear in good working order, staying comfortable and safe in the wilds, and preventing problems when the conditions are less than ideal (as they often are out there).

- **Pro Fix:** While I'm a firm believer in tackling all the problems that I can, I also know that sometimes you have to call in the big guns. The Pro Fix sidebars throughout the book will teach you when to wave the white flag and send something back to the manufacturer or a gear repair shop for a professional fix.

- **Splurge!:** I've also included shopping advice throughout the book. Because at some point it might be time to throw in the towel and splurge on something new. These sidebars will help you make the right buying decisions, based on your trips' needs and your budget.

I'd like to thank the many people who contributed in myriad ways to the building of this book. This was a massive team effort, and I couldn't have done it without the support and help of so many of my friends and colleagues in the outdoor industry. Thanks to Steve Roy, who worked alongside me through many of these repairs, with his camera at the ready. A huge thanks to Meg Erznoznik, who dodged Hurricane Irene and sacrificed the best days of summer to shoot more photos and keep me impeccably organized. For their expertise along the way, thanks to George Farkas, Drew Williams and Bill Gamber from Big Agnes; Julie Parker from Rainy Pass Repair; Chris Felix at CRK Enterprises; Cheriss Faiola and David Wiggs from McNett; Gregg Fischer from Leki; Curtis Graves, Doug Heinrich, and Joe Skivran from Black Diamond; Rick Vance from Petzl; Gary Fraze from Duraflex; Diane Leavy and Kerri Dellasanti from Cascade Designs; Matt Wilson at American Recreation; RJ Hosking and Jess Clayton at Patagonia; Kate McCabe from ZRK Enterprises; Julie Atherton with Steripen; Mike May with Gerber; and Sue Minichiello with DMT.

Thanks to many of my colleagues (past and present) at BACKPACKER: Julia Vandenoever and Genny Fullerton for their photo expertise and perpetual willingness to help; Katie Herrell, Ben Fullerton, Kim Phillips, Andrew Bydlon, and Steve and Jen Howe for donating some of their shots; Dennis Lewon for proofing the final draft; and Jon Dorn for supporting me throughout the project.

A *huge* thanks to all the loyal BACKPACKER readers who entrusted me with their beloved pieces of gear and sent me their awesome stories and photos: Bill Brown, Scott Rohrig, Julie Ellison, Steve Roy, John Fulton, James Dziezynski, Matt Vellone, Melanie Robinson, Abby Baur, Max Katzmartsic, Meg Erznoznik, Mike Browning, Gary Colvard, Rod Goldhahn, Mike Nancarrow, and Paige Boucher. Without you, this book could not have happened.

Thanks to my editor, John Burbidge, for letting me chart my own course. And lastly, thanks to my family: my husband, Shaun, and my two boys, Charlie and Joey, for putting up with all the craziness and for letting me take over the garage for six months, turning it into a giant gear workshop and storage space.

CHAPTER ONE

Setting Up Shop

On day two of a six-day backcountry hike in Arizona's Glen Canyon National Recreation Area, my air mattress sprung a leak. After a crummy night's sleep during which I had to get up and puff air back into my pancake-like pad every two hours, I woke up early and crawled over my thoroughly annoyed tentmate to get to work on the repair. After rummaging through my pack, I realized that I had neglected to pack any repair tools. So I brewed coffee and waited 'til my comrades woke up. Surely one of the seven of us would have a repair kit, right? Wrong. I thought he packed one, he thought she packed one, and so on. The only thing remotely equipped to buy me a little sleep for the remainder of the trip was a few feet of duct tape wrapped around somebody's trekking pole.

That was five years ago, and since then I don't head off into the bush without at least a very basic repair kit. Outdoor shops carry many prepackaged repair kits that will see you through most scrapes, but they often include things that I've never, in almost twenty years of taking backcountry trips, had the need to use (like a hot glue stick, safety pins, and replacement buckles that don't match any of the ones I'm carrying).

So while these kits are a great place to start, it's best to build your own, which can be custom-tailored to work with the gear that you carry. I've got two fix-it kits: an ultralight one designed for backcountry trips, and then my at-home toolbox, which is vast and deep (you'll find all my favorite products and tools throughout this book); it has everything I need to handle big fixes and regular maintenance.

My friend Shannon relaxes atop his inflated pad, while I make do with a stony seat.

Build Your Gear Station

All good gearheads need some real estate in which to work. Not only does it keep you organized for upcoming trips, it provides a perfect place to tinker, fix, store, maintain, and otherwise commune with your gear. Plus, it keeps your stuff consolidated so your spouse won't complain that you're usurping too much basement space.

For all those reasons I built this workbench a few years ago. It only took a few hours and cost not much more than $50. I highly recommend it for any self-respecting gearhead. These general instructions and illustrations will give you the gist of the project. For more detailed instructions and measurements, just troll around on Google for a similar bench . . . they abound on the web.

1. **Build the frame:** Use two-by-fours and build one side at a time, on the floor; it'll be easier to square the joints. Assemble with screws, not nails, for better longevity.

2. **Add the shelves:** Use plywood, not particleboard, for a more durable surface. Install the bottom shelf first. Want a larger working surface? Cut the top to overhang the frame by 6 inches.

3. **Hang some pegboard:** (A) Secure this to the wall studs, not the workbench. Organize your gear and tools to maximize space, using a pegboard accessory kit (you'll find tons of options at a large home improvement store).

4. **Customize your bench:** Create designated spots to hang ice axes, collapsed trekking poles, first-aid kit, ditty bags, rolls of tape, spools of wire, plus tools like hammers and pliers. Rig a shelf (B) off the pegboard and line it with all your gear treatments: washes, boot and fabric DWRs (durable water repellents), and denatured alcohol for cleaning sooty stoves. Use small cardboard boxes for storing webbing, cord scraps, tent stakes, and more. Put those old BPA-laden water bottles

(C) to work storing small items, like spare batteries, first-aid supplies, sunscreen, and lip balm tubes. Install a pair of 6-inch C-clamps or vise grips (D) (one on each end of the bench top) for doing boot-resoling or ski-tuning work. Use the bottom shelf (E) to store packs, tents, bags, and other bulky items. Tape seasonal and trip-specific packing lists (you can print them out at backpacker.com) to the wall for easy reference.

If your gear is scattered all over your house—in various closets, the basement, the garage—build yourself a work station that will let you store it, organize it, and fix it all in one place. Your spouse will surely thank you.

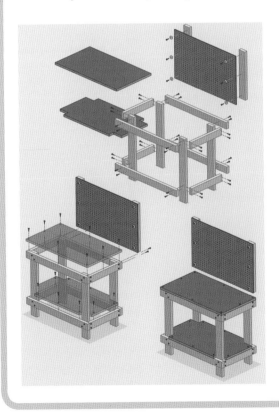

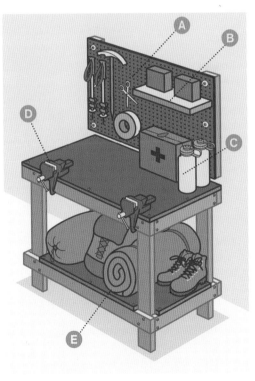

MY BACKCOUNTRY KIT

I custom-tailor this kit based on the type and length of my trip, but these are the basics of my ultralight backpacking repair kit. In the chapters that follow, you'll learn how to use each of these items.

O-rings:
If I'm using a liquid-fuel stove on any given trip, I always pack a few spare O-rings just in case.

Seam Grip:
There are 1,001 uses for this awesome adhesive. I never leave home without a small tube.

Zip-top bag:
No need to get fancy. A freezer-weight zip-top bag is the lightest receptacle for your repair kit, plus it's waterproof and see-through, so you can get at the goods quickly.

Buckles:
Pack a replacement for your pack's hipbelt, a Slik Clip (designed to join any two pieces of webbing), and a ladder lock with a slit (making it easy to install without sewing).

Alcohol prep pads:
I use these to clean any fabric surface before making a repair.

Tent pole repair sleeve:
Tough to improvise and a godsend if you break a pole, this aluminum sleeve is key. I wrap a bit of duct tape around the sleeve, which I'll use to affix the sleeve in place. But I always keep a few more feet of the silver stuff wrapped around my water bottle or trekking pole.

Tear-Aid patches:
This is the best repair tape I've found. Be sure to get "Type A," which works on pretty much all fabrics. ("Type B" adheres only to vinyl.)

Multitool:
I've been using the Leatherman Juice S2 for years. I love it because it's fully featured (with scissors, pliers, and sundry screwdrivers and blades), but at 4.4 ounces, it's light enough that I don't mind carrying it.

CHAPTER TWO

Fabrics

Nylon. Cordura. Polyester. Silnylon. Gore-Tex. Wool. Polartec. Pertex. Where would the outdoor adventurer be without these (and so many other) wonder fabrics? We'd be cold, wet, and miserable, that's where.

And here's the reality: These technical fabrics that are so omnipresent in our clothing, shelters, sleeping bags, and packs are not invincible. Rips happen, and so do holes, seam failures, and leaks, even in the most expensive items.

This chapter will show you how to repair all the major types of fabric found in outdoor gear. The majority of the fixes I'll cover will rely on adhesives of some sort. Why? Because I have minimal patience for sewing and I have no time or desire to add it to my skill set. I only break out the needle and thread for straightforward patch jobs or small, simple repairs on soft items—like fleece, wool, and polyester baselayers (adhesives won't work on these because they need a hard surface on which to stick). If something requires serious needle-and-thread work, I'm sending it off to the pros for a perfect repair.

Waterproof and Smooth-Faced Fabrics

TINY HOLES

These fixes will work on apparel, gaiters, tents, sleeping bag shells, and a whole slew of other items—essentially any synthetic fabric that has a smooth surface.

If a campfire ember lands on your sleeve and burns a hole right through, don't sweat it, just perform this ten-second fix.

Step 1: Clean the area with an alcohol prep pad.

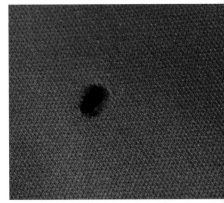

This hole is about as big as the tip of a pencil.

Step 2: Hold a small piece of paper or tape on the backside of the hole to prevent adhesive from seeping through the hole.

Step 3: Smear a dollop of Seam Grip over the hole, smoothing it out with a Popsicle stick, toothpick, or the brush provided (see "Seam Grip Tip" sidebar).

Let the Seam Grip settle into the hole, then smooth it over the fabric so it extends about ¼ inch on all sides.

Step 4: Let it cure for at about eight hours, then remove the backing.

BEFORE YOU START

The first step to any repair involving adhesives is to clean any gunk off the face of the fabric. Those little alcohol prep pads in your first-aid kit work great, or you can use a cotton ball and a bottle of alcohol from your medicine cabinet.

SEAM GRIP TIP

Save the brush that came with your Seam Grip for bigger jobs, like seam-sealing tents and painting along long seams. The reason? Once used, the brush is shot—nothing I've tried (rubbing alcohol, nail polish remover, mineral spirits, etc.) will remove the sticky stuff from the bristles. For small jobs where minimal spreading is required, opt for a Popsicle stick, toothpick, or plastic take-out knife, which do the job just fine and can be wiped clean more easily or tossed in the bin without guilt.

MEDIUM HOLES AND TEARS

Got a hole in your jacket, rain pants, tent, or gaiters? This sew-free technique is so easy it can be done in a matter of minutes in the field.

Step 1: Trim any loose or fraying threads.

It's much easier and cleaner in the end if you take the time to remove little threads.

Step 2: Cut a patch of Tear-Aid or Tenacious Tape that extends at least ¼ inch beyond the edges of the hole. Round the edges of the patch (so they're less prone to peeling). Apply the patch to the inside of the fabric, smoothing it from the center outward to release any air bubbles.

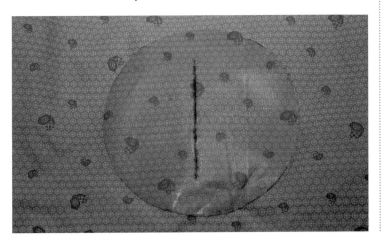

PATCHING INSULATED GARMENTS

This is such an easy repair, you'll feel like you're cheating. The technique is identical to patching a hole in a sleeping bag shell, so refer to Chapter 7 for the full scoop.

Before applying the patch, wipe the surface clean with an alcohol prep pad.

Step 3: Paint the exterior side of the hole with Seam Grip, extending the requisite ¼ to ½ inch beyond the problem area. Let it cure thoroughly. The only drawback of this technique is that when the Seam Grip dries, it's fairly visible—in the form of a slick-looking smear. Personally, I don't mind this.

Run a generous bead of Seam Grip along the tear, then gently smooth it flat.

Step 4: But if you do, consider skipping the Seam Grip and instead using an identical Tenacious Tape or Tear-Aid patch on the front side. Make sure that the centers of each patch bond to each other for maximum durability. This is a great, clean-looking solution for clothing, because both tapes are clear and blend right in with any fabric color.

The clear patch is barely visible on the sleeve of this rain shell.

LINED GARMENTS

Some jackets and pants have free-hanging inner liners that can foil your sewing attempts because you can't flip the fabric over and gain access to the back. But I've recently had luck with this no-sew technique on an old pair of lined rain pants belonging to my husband.

Step 1: Lay the garment out flat (no wrinkles in either the face or the liner fabric!) and trim any fraying threads. Cut a swath of Tenacious Tape or Tear-Aid that will handle the wound, and peel off the backing.

Nylon often tears in an L shape, which makes the repair simple because you just position the flap back in place.

Step 2: Carefully work the patch into the hole/tear with the sticky side up. Though this patch is destined to live between the liner fabric and the face fabric, it will only adhere to the inner surface of the face fabric.

Inserting the patch can be a bit tricky, but the key is to make sure everything is smooth and bubble- and wrinkle-free.

Step 3: When the patch is situated perfectly, press the face fabric into the patch so it adheres. If it's a tear you're working on (as opposed to a hole with fabric missing in the center), rejoin the edges of the tear as closely as possible against the patch.

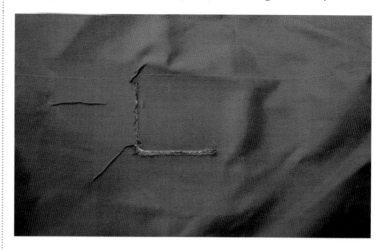

Try to avoid wrinkles in the fabric as shown here, because once the tape is in place, it's very difficult to move. Wrinkles don't affect performance, only cosmetics. In the case of these twenty-year-old rain pants, cosmetics were of little concern.

Step 4: Paint the area with Seam Grip and let it cure overnight.

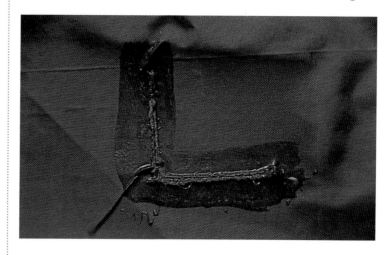

When Seam Grip dries, it will have a glossy sheen.

When your Gore-Tex jacket or tent rainfly gets gashed in the field, it almost never happens at a time when you can immediately stop what you're doing, pull out your repair kit, and make a really solid, permanent repair. (The adhesives required take at least four hours to cure properly.) So don't rush it. You're way better off making a quick, temporary repair that will get you through the trip, and then doing it right back home.

Unless you really have no other option, resist the urge to slap a piece of duct tape over a rip or hole. Yes, it will likely stick for a good long while, but when you peel it off to make the "real" fix, it leaves behind residue that's tough to get off. Instead, patch it with Tear-Aid or Tenacious Tape, which sticks just as well, is equally waterproof, and is a cinch to peel off.

Soft Fabrics

Adhesives don't stick to fuzzy fleeces and wools or stretchy polyester baselayers, which is why good repair gurus need to know a couple of very basic stitches.

STITCHES TO KNOW

Whip Stitch

This no-brainer stitch works well anytime you want to join two edges together or sew on a patch, and it's what I use about 95 percent of the time because it's easy and strong. Just make continuous loops in a tight, uniform line. (*Tip:* Run the stitches diagonally across the seam for a better hold, and work with the garment inside out for the most invisible stitch line.)

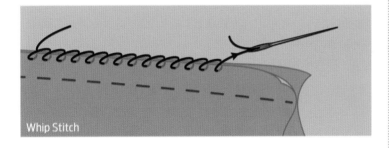

Whip Stitch

Running Stitch

This one works well in areas that are not typically stressed or tensioned, like on the hem of your hiking pants. You simply swoop the threaded needle in and out of the fabric (picture a dolphin jumping in and out of the water). The key: Stitches should be evenly spaced (no more than ¼ inch) and both the underside and the topside should look identical.

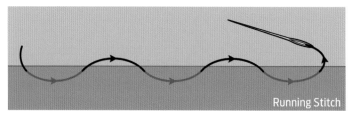
Running Stitch

Back Stitch

This is one of the strongest stitches you can make without a sewing machine. It's ideal for patches that might see some stress (think elbow or knee).

Step 1: Starting at the backside of the fabric, bring the needle down to the front side. Make a small stitch forward (¼ to ½ inch) up through to the backside.

Step 2: For the next move, double halfway back into the first stitch, and come through to the front.

Step 3: Moving up toward the back again, step the next stitch forward. (*Tip:* Make sure each stitch is equal in size. I typically try to make each one about the size of a piece of long-grain rice.)

Step 4: Again, double halfway back through the previous stitch and come down to the front. Continue this way throughout your repair, so that each new stitch you make reinforces the last one.

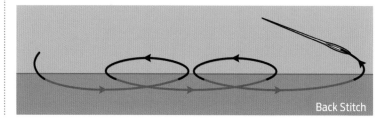
Back Stitch

TYING OFF/FINISHING A SEWING JOB

I've already admitted that I'm sewing-challenged, mostly from a lack of patience, but also, largely, because finishing or tying off even a simple seam has always befuddled me. Then I learned these key tips:

- If using a whip stitch (like I do most of the time), make sure to start to decrease the size of your stitches as you reach the end of the tear. Your new seam should extend about ¼ inch beyond the actual tear and taper down to the tiniest of stitches. This prevents any puckering or bulging at the end of your new seam.

- To tie off any sewing job, just pull the needle through to the back and take a tiny in-and-out stitch of fabric. Pull the needle through 'til you have a loop of thread remaining and place the needle through that loop. Gently pull until a knot forms against the fabric. Then repeat another loop and knot right next to it. Pull to tighten, and snip the thread.

REAL PEOPLE, REAL PROBLEMS: SEWING A TEAR

Bill Brown, a freelance writer from Redding, California, was making a snowboard descent of Mount Shasta on a warm June day while wearing his beloved midweight zip-turtleneck from Icebreaker (pictured). "It was an amazing ride in the summer slush until about halfway to the trailhead when I caught an edge and took a dive down the mountain's face. No major bodily harm done, but while I was cartwheeling, my forearm managed to whack the edge of my board, which resulted in a 1½-inch gash in my sleeve and my arm."

The Fix: A nice, tight whip stitch seam. It doesn't have to be picture-perfect, just functional. In this case, because the fabric had a loose, stretchy weave, I wanted to make sure the seam held, so I doubled back over it, essentially giving it a seam on top of a seam.

This whip stitch may be crude, but it's effective.

Bill Brown loves his wool midlayer from Icebreaker.

Splurge!

Need to amp up the warmth on your next camping trip? Buy a new insulating layer. Consider these pros and cons to find the materials right for you.

INSULATION	PROS	CONS
Down Puffy	Maximum warmth-to-weight ratio; supreme packability; super durable	Wet = useless because feathers flatten and clump; expensive
Synthetic Puffy	Still functions when wet (doesn't lose loft, like down); less expensive than down	Not as warm or packable as down
Fleece	Ideal for warmer-weather insulation or cold-weather midlayer while on the move (it breathes); dries fast	Bulky when packed
Wool	Looks great; sustainably sourced; provides a lot of warmth in a thin layer	Heavyish

FEATURES TO LOOK FOR:

- Well-placed pockets that won't be blocked when you wear your backpack
- Smooth-running zippers
- A tapered, thermally efficient cut that works well with your other layers
- A long, butt-length hem
- A hood (or not, depending on your preference)
- Cuffs that fit your wrist snugly, but without pinching, to prevent drafts
- A hem drawcord so you can stymie drafts from below
- A cozy, snug-fitting neckline with a soft lining that feels good under your chin

Cleaning and Storing

Dirt, sweat, campfire smoke, sunscreen, bug repellent, single malt scotch, and beef stroganoff. These are just a few of the things that inevitably build up on our outdoor clothing. And while proper, regular cleaning is key to making your clothes last and perform their best, here's the rub: Excessive washing will cause premature wear. The key is knowing when a wash is due. If your fleece jacket smells like armpits, or your rain pants are caked with mud from the knee down, it's pretty obvious. Assuming typical, regular usage, consider these guidelines for when to wash. (Of course, if you're an uber-user, you'll have to do it more frequently; if you're an occasional user, dial it back.)

ONCE PER SEASON

- Shell gear (**Note:** Shell gear should also be washed—and treated with a DWR— whenever you discover that it's no longer beading water.)
- Synthetic or down insulated jackets
- Fleece or wool midlayers
- Gloves, hats, and gaiters

AFTER EACH TRIP

- Baselayers
- Socks
- Hiking pants, shorts, and T-shirts

Washing Outdoor Apparel

For starters, invest in a gear-specific cleaner (many are suggested in this chapter). Household detergents are okay in a pinch, but they leave behind residues that can hinder a shell's breathability, a baselayer's wicking ability, or, in the case of wool, make it scratchier. It's not something you'll notice right away, but you're shortchanging yourself over the life of the garment. Follow these tips to get the most out of each wash:

- Make a trip to the laundromat. Big commercial washers and dryers have the volume required to give your gear plenty of breathing room, plus the front-loading washers lack center agitators that can damage garments.
- Check the directions on the label. Typically, you'll want to wash gear with warm or cold water on the gentle cycle, and dry in medium heat.
- Zip all zippers and fasten all Velcro and snaps to prevent any undue abrasion.
- Pretreat any stains with your purpose-built cleaner and let it soak in for a few minutes before beginning the cycle.

These cleaners only end up costing a few bucks per washing.

- Run the washer through an extra rinse cycle (to remove any residue) and spin cycle (to extract water).
- Before you toss any shell gear into the dryer, give it a spray with a DWR treatment (I like ReviveX Spray-On Water Repellent). Pay particular attention to key spots: on the shoulders, along the front zipper, and at the cuffs. These areas tend to wet out faster than others.
- Dry on medium heat until gear is dry to the touch. Any puffy insulated items should also be hung or laid out to air-dry overnight.

PURPOSE-BUILT SOAPS

For Shells
- ReviveX Synthetic Fabric Cleaner
- Nikwax Tech Wash
- Granger's Performance Wash

For Baselayers
- Nikwax Base Wash (any synthetics)
- Nikwax Wool Wash
- ReviveX Wool, Silk, and Bamboo Cleaner
- Granger's Performance Wash

For Down-filled Garments and Sleeping Bags
- Nikwax Down Wash
- ReviveX Down Cleaner
- Granger's Performance Wash

For Synthetic-filled Garments and Sleeping Bags
- ReviveX Synthetic Fabric Cleaner
- Granger's Performance Wash

Removing Pine Sap

Pine sap is one of those things that can be a total pain in the butt if you don't have the right stuff to remove it. If you do have the right stuff and the right techniques, however, it's like wiping up spilled milk. Here are some tips for different types of gear:

- For clothing or other small items: Wait 'til you get home and stick the item in the freezer for a couple of hours until the sap is very hard and crackly. Then crease the sap stain and roll the crease back and forth between your fingers. The sap should break away from the fabric. Gently scrape any residual sap off with a plastic spatula or knife.

- For a sleeping bag or tent (too big for the freezer): Soak a sponge with one of these household items: rubbing alcohol, nail polish remover, or Goo Gone (found at all home improvement stores), and scrub away. Once the sap is gone, clean the fabric with hot water. (*Tip:* Always test a small, hidden area first, to make sure the fabric and/or fabric coatings don't react.)

- For boot leather: Smear the sap with peanut butter (preferably smooth, not crunchy), work it in, and then wash away.

Removing Duct Tape Residue

Let's face it: Sometimes duct tape is all we have on hand to patch a tear. It will do the trick and stick around for the duration of your trip and then some (especially if you round the edges). But when you peel it off, you're left with a gunky residue that doesn't just come out in the wash. I've tried just about everything and found the best results with Goo Gone Spray Gel, an oil-based cleaner found at most home improvement stores. Goo Gone doesn't stain fabric and doesn't seem to affect its performance. WD-40 works almost as well, while Goof-Off and Jigaloo stain fabric. But you be the judge (see photo above, right).

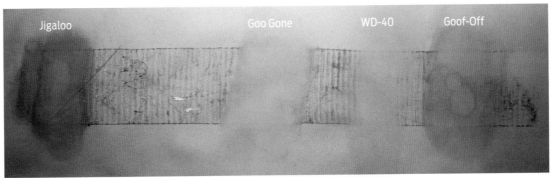

Jigaloo   Goo Gone   WD-40   Goof-Off

I tried cleaning duct tape residue with four different products. As the photo above shows, the results vary considerably.

GUNKED-UP VELCRO

Have you ever looked really closely at Velcro? (If not, check it out on almost any shell jacket you have in your closet.) The generic name for this ubiquitous fastener is "hook and loop," and a close inspection will show you why: The fuzzy (aka "loop") side of the tape is made of a tangled nest of whorled fibers. The scratchy (aka "hook") side has tight rows of miniature plastic fishhooks. When joined, the hooks grab onto the loops for dear life, and you've got the perfect seal for any type of cuff.

With serious use, the hook side of the Velcro can get clogged with lint, fibers, dirt, and other debris, which inhibits its ability to form a good seal. If your Velcro starts to look like a miniature lint tray, try these tricks to clean the gunk out:

· Carefully comb through the hooks using a needle or pin.

· Scrub the hooks using a dry toothbrush.

· When machine-washing any item with Velcro, make sure both sides are joined. Not only will this prevent stuff from accumulating, it will protect face fabrics from scratching on the hooks.

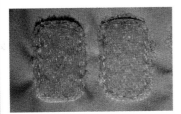

This is the loop side. . .

and these are the hooks.

Pluck debris from the hooks. (Debris doesn't typically collect in the loops.)

Splurge! Ready for a shell upgrade? If so, consider these features.

CHOOSE THIS ...	OR THAT
Hardshell: For the most absolute rain protection in the lightest possible package	**Softshell:** Generally more breathable and stretchier for more freedom of movement, but often heavier
Hooded: Key for hikers and backpackers or anyone who may be out in sustained rain; check for snug adjustments and good peripheral vision	**Hoodless:** Fine for runners and bikers
Full-zip style: Easy on and off; most versatile in terms of venting	**Anorak:** Great protection with a slight weight and packed size savings
Pit zips: Long underarm vents that let you dump heat during high-aerobic activities	**Pocket vents:** Mesh-lined pockets (when left open) aren't as effective as pit zips, but they'll save you a bit of money and pack weight
Pack-friendly pockets: Placed slightly high, so that they remain accessible when you're wearing a pack hipbelt	**Lower handwarmer pockets:** More comfortable for casual, everyday use
Velcro wrist cuffs: Create a tight, weatherproof seal that is adjustable to fit over gloves and different types of layers	**Elastic cuffs:** Often on lighter, less expensive jackets; allow you to push sleeves up your arms for quick air-conditioning while on the move.

CHAPTER THREE

Zippers

Talk to any warranty department or any gear fix-it shop, and they'll tell you that, without any shred of a doubt, zipper failures are the most common problem that befalls hiking gear and apparel. It's not surprising when you think about all the times you've probably yanked mercilessly at your various zippers: like trying to get out of your bag at 3 a.m. with a bursting bladder . . . or desperate to get the tent door closed quickly after diving through a cloud of mosquitoes . . . or forcing a zipper on an overloaded pack pocket. These scenarios usually happen when a tiny flap of fabric gets caught in the slider's path. Modern day zippers are tough, but they're not immune to repeated yanking.

With every tug the slider gets slightly misshapen: The top and bottom pieces begin to open slightly so they don't mesh the coils when they pass over them, and the little separator bar in the bowels of the slider also takes some wear. Many times worn sliders can be pinched back into place using needle-nose pliers (see "Real People, Real Problems," this chapter). But this is generally a temporary fix and a sign that the slider will eventually need to be replaced.

On jackets, zippers provide critical venting options.

Zippers 101
Learn these terms to help you troubleshoot your own zipper problems.

Coil Zipper

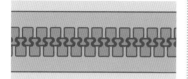

Tooth Zipper

COIL ZIPPER

These have a continuous wrap of nylon filament, which inter-lock as the slider is passed over. Coil zips are generally more lightweight than tooth zips, and are available in waterproof versions. Coil zips also wear more gradually than tooth zips, so you're less likely to have catastrophic failure in the field.

TOOTH ZIPPER

Also called Vislon zippers, these have individual blocks of nylon that interlock as the slider is passed over. Tooth zippers are ex-tremely rugged, but slightly bulkier and heavier than coils. And if a tooth does crack off, the zipper is immediately shot, with no hope for repair—only replacement.

ZIPPER ANATOMY

- **Separating zipper:** Zippers that come apart at both ends (like on a jacket)
- **Nonseparating zipper:** Zippers that are fused on each end (like on a pack pocket or duffle bag)
- **Slider:** The small mechanism that passes over the zipper to align and join the two sides
- **Tape:** The fabric on either side of the zipper
- **Pull:** The grab-tab that attaches to the slider
- **Stop:** Small plastic blocks at each end of the zipper that prevent the slider from coming off the tape
- **Retainer box:** On separating zippers only; the box at the bottom of the slider side that accepts the insertion pin
- **Insertion pin:** On separating zippers only; the squarish pin at the bottom of the non-slider side that fits into the retainer box

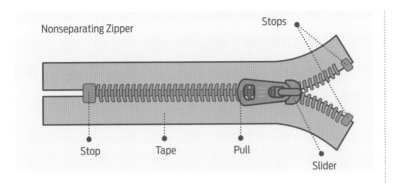

Nonseparating Zipper

Stops

Stop Tape Pull Slider

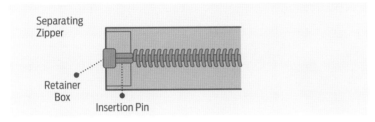

Separating Zipper

Retainer Box

Insertion Pin

Prevention

We've all been there: A piece of fabric or grit gets caught in the slider and we're rushing to move on so we yank, maybe gently at first, but eventually with more force until the slider succumbs and the zipper is zipped. You may think this is a small victory, but keep it up and the slider will get its revenge in the end.

The best thing you can do for your zippers is not yank! If it gets jammed, stop manhandling it. Inspect it to determine the problem. Then remove the problem—in many cases this means gently pulling the fabric out of the slider, not the other way around.

A note on waterproof zippers: These have become very popular on lightweight jackets and pants and backpacks. It's easy to see why: Since the zipper tape is coated with water-proofing, designers can forgo using storm flaps, which saves weight and makes for a very clean look—both of which are great selling points. But sliders don't always play well with waterproof coatings. They tend to grab more frequently, which usually results in the frustrating tug-of-war described on page 25.

Your best bet is to keep waterproof zippers well lubed, using a purpose-built product like McNett Zip Care. It's a liquid lubricant and cleaner in one. First, use a dry toothbrush to remove any visible debris. Then lightly brush the lubricant onto both sides of the zipper and make a few passes with the slider—you should immediately notice less friction and a smoother slide.

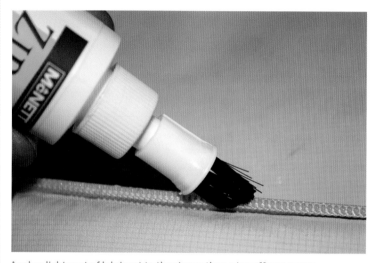

Apply a light coat of lubricant to the zipper, then wipe off any excess.

REAL PEOPLE, REAL PROBLEMS: PINCHING A WORN SLIDER

Scott Rohrig, from Centennial, Colorado, had been using his Mountainsmith fanny pack for a good ten years before the burly front pocket zipper finally gave way to a decade of yanking. "I was headed for the summit of Wheeler Peak (13,161 feet) in New Mexico. I unzipped it to grab my camera and it never closed again. Six years have passed and this little workhorse has languished in my basement. If I'd known it was such an easy fix, I would have done it a long time ago!"

The Fix: After years of use the slider was slightly misshapen—the top and bottom had opened up enough so that they didn't weave the coils together. A simple (but strong) squeeze with needle-nose pliers had it back in the race. (*Tip:* Back the zipper all the way up into the open position, then squeeze one side at a time, gently at first. Keep trying the zipper to see if it closes, and then apply increasing pressure as needed. Be sure to apply equal pressure to both sides of the slider, and be gentle with it from here on out: Eventually that slider will need replacement, but this trick can eke some more life out of it.)

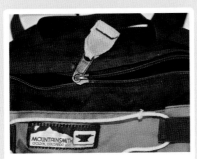

A common problem with an easy, albeit temporary fix.

Worn or stretched-out sliders can often be coerced back into shape with needle-nose pliers.

Scott Rohrig poses with his fanny pack in Great Sand Dunes National Park, Colorado.

Replacing a Slider

If a slider is toast—meaning that you can't fix it by pinching it closed—you'll have to remove it from the zipper track before replacing it, and removing it is sometimes the trickiest part

Before you remove a slider, make a note of the size, so you can get the proper replacement. Zippers come in many different brands and sizes; the size is usually engraved on the back of the slider. The most common sizes for outdoor gear and apparel range from 3 (smaller zippers found on lightweight jackets, for instance) up to 10 (big, beefy ones found on packs and sleeping bags).

This is a #5 tooth—or Vislon—slider.

SEPARATING ZIPPERS

It's fairly straightforward to replace a slider on a separating zipper (like those found on jackets or sleeping bags), because you have easy access to the top of the zipper tape and don't need to rip any seams to extricate the bad slider. All you need are a few tools (wire cutters and needle-nose pliers) and a new top stop (you can find them at any sewing shop for pennies).

Step 1: Using a pair of wire cutters, crack off the top stop.

Step 2: Slide the damaged slider off the track.

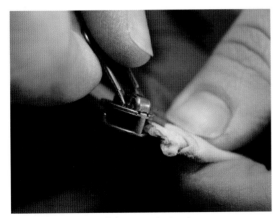

Step 3: Slip the new slider onto the track.

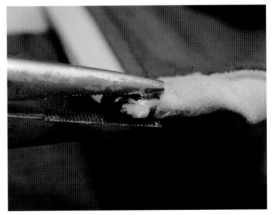

Step 4: Finish the repair by crimping on a new top stop with your needle-nose pliers.

NONSEPARATING ZIPPERS

It's trickier to remove a slider on a nonseparating zipper because the ends are sewn into the item and often covered with binding tape. But it's still possible to remove and replace a slider on a nonseparating zipper without creating a pesky sewing job.

Smaller zippers can often be easily pried off with a flat-head screwdriver. Just work the head of the screwdriver under one of the "wings" or into the rear opening and try to pop it off. Be careful not to gouge yourself—it sometimes takes a little force. If it doesn't want to give using just a screwdriver, don't risk damaging the zipper's coils or teeth; move on to the next option.

Medium-size to large zippers require specialized tools. The best option is a pair of carpenter's pincers, which can easily bite through even the beefiest zippers.

A super-simple method for replacing a slider on a nonseparating zipper entails using a smart device called a Flip an Zip (flipanzip.com), which comes in a variety of sizes to fit most any zipper. It's a two-piece metal slider that thumbscrews into place on the zipper track—coil or tooth. You simply place the Flip an Zip slider over the two sides of the zipper and tighten the thumbscrew. Then attach the included zipper pull and you're back in business.

Tip: Many modern zippers are reversed, so the coils are less exposed to the elements and the backside of the zipper faces outward. In these cases the Flip an Zip can be installed with the thumbscrew on the inside—it's a bit trickier to manage, but totally doable with a touch of patience.

The only downsides to the Flip an Zip solution are that it's a tad heavier than normal sliders and it's not as aesthetically pleasing as they only come in a no-nonsense metal finish.

You can often just pry off a bad slider on smaller-size zippers.

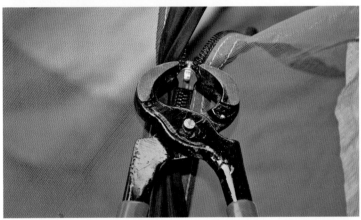

For larger zippers cut through the center post of the slider using a pincer tool.

Install the Flip an Zip slider.

Fixing a Misaligned Tooth

If a tooth on a Vislon zipper cracks off in the field, you're out of luck, and it's time to get creative to come up with a way to keep your jacket fastened for the remainder of the trip. But sometimes a tooth just becomes misaligned a bit, like it did on my son's favorite fleece jacket. In cases like this all it takes is a gentle pinch with the pliers to realign the teeth. If the tooth cracks off during your attempt, well, you gave it a shot. But now you'll need to have the whole zipper replaced.

Sometimes an individual tooth will not mesh properly with its mate on the other side. When that happens, you can't move the slider beyond that spot.

Lightly pinch the crooked tooth back into place.

CHAPTER FOUR

Backpacks

A major pack blowout is a rare occurrence. But if it does happen when you're miles into the sticks . . . man, you'd better know what to do or you could be in for a long, painful hike home. For the most part the fixes you'll be faced with in the pack department are ones that are innocuous at first—fraying webbing, abrasion on the packbag, small tears in mesh or stretch-woven pockets—but if left unattended, they could eventually spell doom for your beloved load hauler. This chapter will teach you how to spot those potential trouble spots, nip them in the bud, and keep your pack doing what it's supposed to do: schlep your gear. You'll also learn what to do in the field if a major accident does strike your pack—like a busted buckle or big gash.

Back to those innocuous little glitches: Packbags endure so much daily abuse. We drop them, fully loaded, on rocks and sticks. We sit on them. We haul them up sandstone cliffs. We shimmy though rocky crevices. We stuff their pockets with sharp, hard-edged tools. We overstuff them, then reef on the zipper to get them closed. For me, rarely does a trip go by that I don't inflict some sort of little wound to my backpack.

Packbag Wounds

If you want a good, long relationship with your pack, spend a few minutes at the end of each trip giving it a good once-over, paying careful attention to the pack bottom and any mesh pockets, which tend to abrade easily. So many major problems can be curtailed in their infant stages with Seam Grip. Here are just two examples of where I've "stopped the bleeding" and fixed my packs to go on to serve me for many more trips.

By carefully loading your pack to cushion sharp objects inside, you can prevent abrasion on the pack fabric.

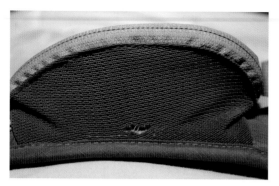

This mesh hipbelt pocket lies atop a hard plastic sheet inside the hipbelt, which has rubbed through the mesh, creating a small hole.

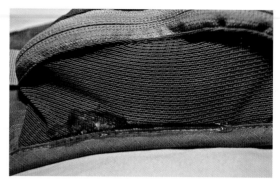

THE FIX: A good smear of Seam Grip plugs the hole and reinforces the mesh.

PACK TLC

Toss your pack around like a gym bag and it will meet an early demise. Treat it lovingly and it will be with you for the long haul. One key tip for preserving the integrity of the shoulder straps and their stitching: Always lift it by the haul loop just below the top lid. That's what the loop is there for. If your pack is too heavy, get help from a hiking partner or prop it on a truck tailgate or log. Or lift it using a simple method that protects both your pack and your spine: Bend one leg into a shallow lunge, then pick up the pack by the haul loop and place it on your front, bent thigh, making sure the shoulder straps are facing you. With one hand still on the haul loop, twist your torso and slide one arm through the far shoulder strap, then bend forward to shift the weight onto your back and slide the other arm through the strap.

Pick up your heavy pack properly and you'll preserve both your pack and your back.

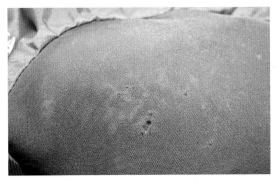

This stretchy woven side pocket—made of a very tightly woven mesh—has suffered some abrasion wear.

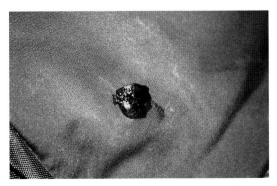

THE FIX: A gob of Seam Grip stops the bleeding and prevents further abrasion in this area.

Buckles

According to my very unscientific research, the average backpack has about ten buckles. The most critical one on any pack is, without a doubt, the hipbelt side-release buckle. If you're carrying a forty-pound load and your hipbelt cracks off, you're in for a world of pain if you don't know how to fix it, or at least jury-rig it so you can bear that pack weight on your hips.

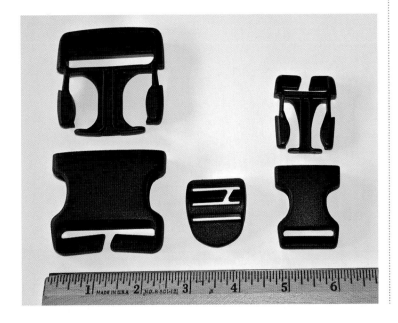

Left to right: Hipbelt side-release buckles are typically 1 to 2 inches; ladder-lock or tension buckles (commonly found on shoulder straps) are almost always 1 inch; compression and top-lid side-release buckles are generally 1 inch.

REAL PEOPLE, REAL PROBLEMS: SEWING A TEAR

Julie Ellison, gear editor at *Climbing* magazine, bought her Kelty daypack as a freshman in college. Aside from hauling books for four years, she's carried it up countless peaks during seasonal rangering stints in Yellowstone and Glacier National Parks, and used it as her around-town "purse" for more than seven years. "The 1,000+ miles have taken their toll," she says. "The mesh pockets have a smattering of annoying holes that render the side pockets useless. I've moved on to more technical packs for hiking, but I still want this pack to use as my carry-on for flights. It's like an old friend."

The open-weave mesh side pockets on this daypack were riddled with holes.

The Fix: First, I tied the end of my sewing thread in an overhand knot through the mesh. Then I just pinched the edges of the mesh together and began whip-stitching them closed. I used wide stitches to be sure that I grabbed the undamaged strands of mesh—it's better to have a pinched or puckered seam than have your work rip out because you didn't go wide enough to bring the healthy mesh into the seam. It may not be a work of art, but short of sending the pack in to get the entire pocket replaced (which would be costly), it's effective and will eke many more miles out of the pack as long as Julie doesn't load the pocket with anything too sharp or heavy.

Patience and some simple stitching pulled all the torn edges together to make the pocket whole again.

Julie Ellison bagging Avalanche Peak in Wyoming with her trusty Kelty daypack.

You can easily avoid a jury-rig situation (which is sure to be only marginally comfortable, at best) by packing a mere ounce of antidote. First, measure a few key buckles on your pack.

Once you know these dimensions, be sure to stock replacements in your backcountry repair kit. Buy the buckle type that's designed for quick and easy field repair. They have slots that allow you to replace the broken buckle in a matter of seconds without having to cut and sew webbing, and they can literally save your butt in the event of a blowout.

REPLACING A BROKEN LADDER LOCK

These buckles are often found on shoulder straps, compression straps, and many other places where webbing needs to be tightened down around the pack. After ten-plus years of use, the ladder lock on the shoulder strap of my favorite North Face Base Camp Duffel broke, which meant that I couldn't carry the big beast (which often weighs fifty pounds when fully loaded with gear) backpack style. That just wouldn't do, so I replaced the ladder lock in a matter of three minutes.

Step 1: Remove the broken buckle. If it's not a threaded tension buckle that you can simply unthread, you'll have to cut through the plastic bar that holds the webbing loop. Just be patient and use cutters at home or the sharpest knife in your group if in the field, taking care not to slice through the webbing (because then you'll have to resort to sewing).

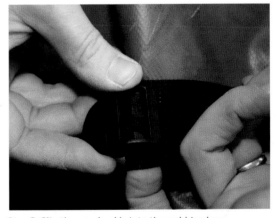

Step 2: Slip the new buckle into the webbing loop.

USING A SLIK CLIP

This is a handy little buckle to have in your backcountry repair kit. The beauty of a Slik Clip is that you can join any two pieces of 1-inch webbing without sewing, which can come in handy if any of your pack straps break, or if you need to create a haul loop or hang items from your pack.

Slik Clips have two arms that open wide so you can easily insert the webbing, then snap the clip shut, securing the webbing in place.

Ultralight Packs

Anyone hell-bent on slashing their pack weight knows that frameless UL (ultralight) packs are the way to go. They can weigh as little as eight ounces for a 2,500-cubic-inch pack (typical overnight size), but their wispy fabrics—often silnylon—require some special TLC. Don't expect to be able to toss it around, scrape it against rocks, or haul it up a cliff without damaging the fabric.

Any gash that crops up on a silnylon pack can be patched using the same patching techniques explained in Chapter 2. Just be sure to use SilNet adhesive (Seam Grip won't stick), and for bigger holes a good adhesive patch like Tear-Aid or Tenacious Tape.

If your silnylon pack starts to show some light wear and

tear, or if you just want to apply some preventative insurance on high-wear areas—like the pack bottom, for instance—buy a couple tubes of SilNet. Using a foam brush, paint a thin coat of the adhesive over the area in question. SilNet is tough stuff and will stunt the growth of any pilling, or prevent it before it starts. Of course, painting large swaths of the fabric will add a touch of weight to the pack, but it's pretty minimal.

Cleaning and Storing

Packs are low-maintenance items. You don't need fancy soaps or special equipment, and it's rare that you'd ever need to treat it with a DWR to help it repel water. But your pack does need a good scrubbing every once in a while. If you neglect this chore, your pack will eventually become a magnet for squirrels, mice, raccoons, and other critters who are well-known for chewing through even tough, 1,000-denier Cordura to get to a few crumbs from your Clif bar, or gnawing and sucking on the salty sweat deposits that can build up in your shoulder straps.

Even daily users won't have to wash their packs more than once a season. If you use it less frequently, you could go a few years between scrubdowns. But when the time comes, here's what to do:

- Remove all the grit from the bottom of the pack and the corners of the pockets. Use a vacuum to suck tiny crumbs from hard-to-reach seam areas.
- Get a big bucket of warm water mixed with a healthy squirt of mild dish soap (like Joy or Palmolive). Using a plastic-bristled vegetable brush, get to work and give it some serious elbow grease. Pay particular attention to the areas of the pack that come in contact with your sweaty body: the shoulder straps, the hipbelt, and any back padding.
- Use your garden hose to give it a high-powered rinse.
- Hang it in the shade (to protect it from UV damage) until it's totally dry.

WEBBING TIP

Any time you have to cut webbing, use a lighter to heat-seal the cut edge so it won't fray down the road.

Heat-seal webbing with a blast of flame.

Tips from the Field: Backpacks

- **Load it up:** Properly packing your backpack means a more balanced load and easy access to all your stuff. Place your heaviest gear close to your spine at around lumbar level (not too high or the pack will get tippy). Insulate poky or delicate stuff in the center of the pack, where it won't rip the bag or get smushed. And pack frequently used items—snacks, sunscreen, water treatment—either in the top lid, side pockets, or hipbelt pockets, so you don't have to stop and drop your pack to reach them.

PACK FITTING 101

If you do decide to splurge on a new pack, getting the right fit is absolutely key. Here are a few tips to get you sized correctly. (Also check out backpacker.com: There are lots of great visuals—videos and slideshows.)

1. Load the pack with at least 20 pounds. Why? Because an empty pack always feels good, plus, without some weight in it, you won't get a sense of how it rests on your hips and settles into the shape of your spine.

2. Put on the pack. Snug the hipbelt and shoulder straps slightly. Check to make sure the overall torso length is comfortable and shorten/lengthen to taste.

3. Check the shoulder straps: Properly sized, there should be no gap atop the shoulders, and the load lifter anchor point should be at collarbone level.

4. Check the hipbelt: The padding should be level with your pelvic shelf and reach far forward enough that your hipbones are covered.

5. Once the basic torso length, hipbelt, and shoulder strap length is dialed in, snug the hipbelt stabilizer straps, which pull the pack into your lumbar area.

6. Snug the load lifter straps and sway your shoulders back and forth to test the pack's stability. The pack should stay close to your body, move with your body, and not pitch you off balance in any way.

7. Fasten the sternum strap. Position it properly between chest and collarbone level. If it's is too low, it will restrict chest expansion and breathing, but when positioned correctly, it will keep the shoulder straps from slipping outward during scrambles and still let you breathe deeply.

- **Hydration compatible:** Most packs these days come with an integrated sleeve along the inside of the packbag that accepts hydration reservoirs. If yours doesn't, don't sweat it. You can still use a hydration system; it just requires more careful packing. Lay the pack flat (with the shoulder straps and hipbelt on the ground). Slip the reservoir inside and position it along the spine. Load your pack in this prone position, until the rest of your gear holds the reservoir in place. Then stand the pack up and keep on packing.

One of the benefits of hauling a big pack: It makes a fine backrest at lunch stops.

- **Always adjust:** Backpacks have all those straps for a reason, and you'll be most comfortable (especially with heavy loads) if you learn how to optimize them.
  - **Load lifters:** Loosen them to settle the weight back down into your lumbar area. When your hips get tired or you need better stability for a scramble, cinch them back up and pull the upper pack closer in to your spine.
  - **Shoulder straps:** Similar to load lifters, shoulder straps allow you to settle the weight firmly onto your hips (loosen them) or bring more of the load onto your shoulders (tighten them). For best results with a big load, keep shifting the weight around during the course of the day, so no one area gets too worked over.
  - **Sternum strap:** Pull it tight to relieve any pressure created by the outsides of the shoulder straps rubbing in the armpit area.
  - **Lumbar strap:** Positioned at the back of the hipbelt, this is a very subtle adjustment that brings the lower load closer into your spine.
- **Rain protection:** In light to moderate rain, your pack will likely repel water, but if serious, prolonged rain is a possibility, consider bringing either a specialized pack cover (it's elasticized around the rim of the opening so it pops over the pack and stays put) or a big garbage bag you can jury-rig.

CRITTER CONCERNS

Don't store food in your pack at night and leave the pack sitting on the ground where hungry little critters (or bigger ones) can nibble their way in. Learn the art of bear-bagging: Suspend your food bag (or the entire pack, by its haul loop) from a sturdy branch at least 10 feet off the ground. Learn more details at backpacker.com.

Splurge!

When you've exhausted all efforts and it's time to buy a new pack, consider these features, as well as the pros and cons of each to help you make the best purchase. Fit is critical with packs, so talk to a knowledgeable salesperson who can measure your torso and help you zero in on packs designed for your shape and size.

PICK THIS . . .	OR THAT
Top loader: Accesses through the top—fewer zippers, less weight, and fewer potential failure points; plus, easier to overstuff	**Panel loader:** Accesses from the top and through curved zippers on the pack body—maximum organization and gear access
Fixed suspension: No torso length adjustment, so a good fit is imperative; saves weight and creates a super-stable carry.	**Adjustable suspension:** Offers the ability to fine-tune fit; often works well for people with torso lengths that fall outside of the average (17 to 20 inches)
Fixed lid: Permanently attaches to pack-bag to minimize weight	**Floating lid:** Attaches via adjustable straps, allowing you to stack gear higher and secure bulky items (rope, rainfly, pads) underneath
Trampoline back: Mesh panel suspended from the frame lets air flow between pack body and your back—great for hot temps and heavy sweaters	**Foam back:** Padded panel cushions your back and keeps load close to the body for maximum agility—but can be hot
Internal frame: Integrated framesheet and/or stays keeps load close to the body; streamlined design allows freedom of movement while scrambling	**External frame:** Packbag suspended off an exterior frame allows good airflow on hot days and a more upright walking posture on trails; too wobbly and wide for scrambling and bushwhacking
Alpine packbag: Single, streamlined compartment with minimal pockets saves weight and boosts agility for climbing, skiing, and scrambling	**Trail packbag:** Plentiful pockets and lash-on points maximize organization and convenience; shorter, wider shape provides for a lower center of gravity and long trail comfort

CHAPTER FIVE

Tents

Your home away from home may be made of wispy nylon and slender aluminum poles, but it gives you critical protection from wind, rain, sun, and snow. Tents endure plenty of stress in their battle against the elements, and mishaps are common. This chapter will give you all the info you need to keep your tent in fighting shape, with fixes for the most common problems and tips for extending its longevity.

Tears

FABRIC

Tears in the field are so common. Hearing that little *pfffft* (yes, that is the sound nylon makes when ripping) while you're setting up your tent in a rainstorm is scary. You immediately picture yourself shivering, wet, and totally bummed out for the duration of the trip. But don't sweat it. The key is to stop the bleeding quickly by slapping on a self-adhesive patch, which, if you're careful, and smart about using your tent in the future, should last you indefinitely. It takes mere minutes.

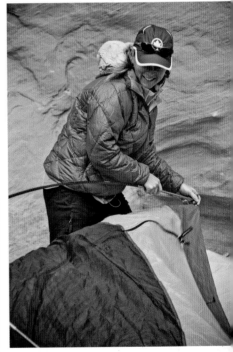

Setting up a tent in Capitol Reef National Park.

This L-shaped tear on the tent's floor (pencil shown for scale) happened when the tent was pitched on a sharp rock.

49

Step 1: If you're making this repair at home, start by ironing the fabric to create the smoothest surface for the patch.

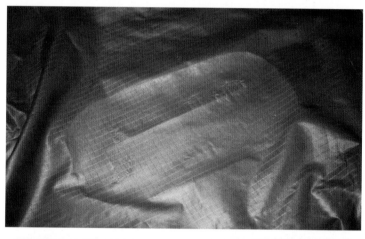

Step 2: Place a patch of Tear-Aid over the gash (on the inside) and smooth out any air bubbles. Round the edges of the patch and make sure they extend at least ½ inch beyond the tear.

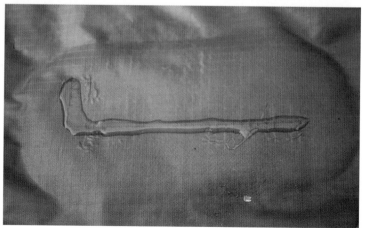

Step 3: Use SilNet (for siliconized nylon) or Seam Grip (for polyurethane-coated nylon) to seal the outside of the repair. Let cure overnight.

REAL PEOPLE, REAL PROBLEMS: BIG HOLES

Steve Roy, from Milton, Massachusetts (one of the photographers for this book), bought his GoLite Lair silnylon tarp after he hiked the Appalachian Trail in 1998 and learned a little something about going ultralight. "One night I was hunkered down through a fantastic thunderstorm in the Lincoln Woods of New Hampshire when a huge gust of wind tore out one of the stakes, and the tarp blew against my gas lantern, melting a large hole in the side of it."

Steve Roy poses with his tarp near his top-secret fishing stash deep in the mountains of New Hampshire.

The Fix: I cleaned the surface with rubbing alcohol and laid the tarp out flat. I measured the hole (3x3 inches) and realized that I'd need to overlap two Tear-Aid patches (they measure 6x3 inches each) in order to completely cover the hole by at least ½ inch all around. Once the two patches were affixed, I flipped the tarp over and applied two more overlapping patches to the other side, pressing the two sticky surfaces together in the middle. For added protection I used a bit of SilNet around the circumference of each patch to ensure the edges don't peel up over time.

Use overlapping patches to mend large holes like this one.

MESH

Snags, tears, and holes in delicate mesh tent walls are oh-so-common. And they can seem pretty innocuous. After all, your rainfly covers the mesh walls, right? But then bug season strikes. And you can be damn sure that every no-see-um, mosquito, and black fly within a 1-mile radius will find that little portal and spend the night torturing you and feasting on your weary flesh.

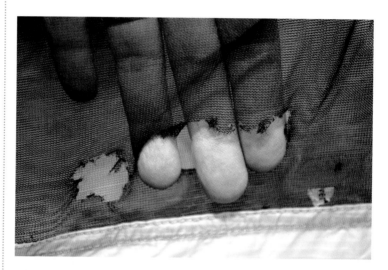

This is what happens when you leave a granola bar in your tent pocket when you go out for a hike. A critter chewed right through the mesh canopy and devoured the bar.

The fix is easy and permanent, using back-to-back MSR Micromesh adhesive patches and a ring of Seam Grip.

Lucky for us, the fix is a snap, and you can easily make a permanent repair in the field. I love the MSR Micromesh Maintenance Kit (msrgear.com). It comes with six oval adhesive patches made of a very fine mesh, perfect for tent walls. Just place one patch on the inside of the hole and place a second patch on the outside, adhesive to adhesive. I found that the patches don't stick perfectly, so I applied Seam Grip to the perimeter for a perfect bond.

MSR's Micromesh Maintenance Kit is the secret to fast, easy, permanent mesh repairs.

Poles

BROKEN POLE

A snapped pole doesn't have to mean disaster, but it can if you don't have two simple items in your repair kit: an aluminum pole sleeve and duct tape. When you get back home, call the manufacturer for a replacement (either the whole pole or a single section), but this fix will last quite a while if you're careful and a little bit lucky (no massive windstorms or snow loads to stress the repair).

The end piece on the pole of my beloved old North Face Tadpole snapped clear in two. (**Note:** The shock cord that threads the pole sections together stops at the beginning of that section in this particular tent. In many tents the shock cord runs all the way to the end of the last pole segment, in which case this broken piece would still be attached via the cord. Either way, the fix is the same.)

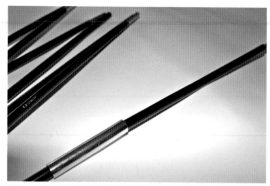

Step 1: Slip the repair sleeve over the pole until it is centered over the broken point. (*Tip:* Be sure to check the diameter of your tent's poles and stock the proper repair sleeve. They come in several different sizes. If the sleeve is too narrow, it won't fit over your pole; if it's too wide, the repair isn't as clean and functional.)

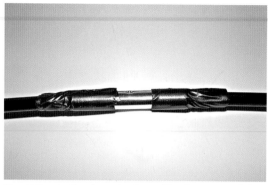

Step 2: Secure the sleeve in place with a few wraps of duct tape over each end. There's no need to overdo it; three to four wraps is enough.

PREVENT POLE PROBLEMS

It's fun to whip your poles around and watch them snap magically together, but it's not fun for your poles—it can damage the pole ends and eventually lead to a split. Instead, carefully place sections together, making sure that the male end is completely inserted into the female end. Also, when breaking your poles down, start with a middle section and work toward the ends: It reduces stress on the shock cord.

When erecting your tent, check that each pole section is tightly and completely fitted together, like this . . .

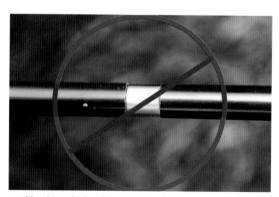

not like this, which will lead to breakage at the female end.

REAL PEOPLE, REAL PROBLEMS: REPLACING SHOCK CORD

John Fulton, from Greenville, South Carolina, has had his Kelty Vortex 2 for about ten years. "It's been a good friend on many a backpacking trip—from weeklong treks through the high country of Rocky Mountain National Park to countless weekend adventures in the Great Smokies, Pisgah National Forest, and the backcountry around Mount Mitchell. But the shock cord in the poles just kept getting weaker over the years. Now each section has to be manually fitted together. By the time I get a pole fitted together and one end secured into the grommet, the sections on the other side would fall apart—a total pain in the butt when it's pitch black and the storm clouds are rolling in!"

The Fix: I popped off the pole tips (sometimes you can do it by hand, sometimes you'll need pliers) and untied the old shock cord, which was totally shot and had no resilience left. Next, I knotted the old cord with new cord of a similar diameter (available at any outdoor shop) and pulled the

John Fulton winter hut camping along the Appalachian Trail in Great Smoky National Park.

old stuff out of the opposite end, threading the entire length of the pole without having to go section by section. When the new cord was threaded, I removed the old, and pulled the new cord to the proper tension. (**Note:** This requires a bit of experimenting. You want to pull the cord tight enough that the sections go together smoothly, but not so tight that the poles are stressed.) Finally, I reinserted the pole tip and John was back in business.

Step 1: Remove the pole tip from one end and untie the cord.

Step 2: Knot the old cord with the new cord, so you can easily pull the new cord through the pole.

Step 3: Once the pole is rethreaded, discard the old cord and reknot the new one onto the pole tip.

Step 4: Trim off any excess and reinsert the pole tip.

Zippers

Tent zippers are notoriously troublesome. With all that mesh and nylon and zippers that often run in circular shapes, snagging is common. And what do most of us do when a snag occurs? We yank. And what happens when we yank? The sliders get worn. When this happens, tent doors won't close, in which case we might as well be sleeping under a tarp.

You could send that tent back to the manufacturer for a slider replacement and a nice, clean repair. But that could take weeks and more bucks than you want to spend, so try tackling it yourself. Before you begin, make sure you have the proper replacement slider. Your best bet is to call the manufacturer and order a replacement (they'll usually send it for free) or invest in the Zipper Rescue Kit (zipperrescue.com), which has a slew of common slider sizes, plus some other zipper parts that are useful. (**Note:** This is an intimidating repair for even die-hard DIYers, but I've done it on several tents, so I promise you it can be done with some patience!)

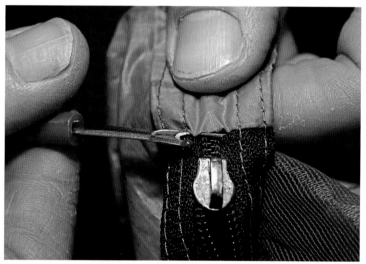

Step 1: Using a seam ripper, open up just enough of the seam so that you can free the end of the zipper tape.

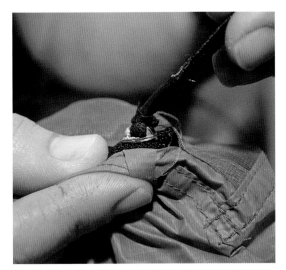

Step 2: Slip both of the worn sliders off the tape. Be sure to note their direction and orientation, so you can replicate it when installing the new sliders. If at all possible, try to get the zipper to engage behind the worn sliders, so that when you remove them, the two sides are joined. This makes the reinstallation much easier.

Step 3: Insert the first slider onto the zipper tape so that both sides are equally inside the slider. If the zipper has remained engaged (as noted in step 2), you'll only be able to insert it up to a point, because the joined coils will prevent it from going farther. At this point insert a seam ripper or needle into one of the two openings and pry apart the engaged coils.

Step 4: Once you feel it give way, the slider will easily move up the zipper tape. Then install the second slider (this one goes on easily).

Step 5: Using small back stitches, sew the fabric back up. Remember, it's not a beauty contest. You just need to get it all back together again. I applied a thin layer of Seam Grip over the inside of my entire sewing job as added reinforcement.

Waterproofing Seams

Believe it or not, a few minuscule pinholes along a seam in your nylon tent can cause leakage issues, which is why the majority of tents sold today come with factory-taped seams on the rainfly and floor. This tape covers up the hundreds of tiny needle holes made by sewing machines when they join two pieces of fabric together.

Most tents will be ready to use the minute you walk out of a store, and for the most part, if you take good care of your tent, the seam tape will never fail you. But there are a couple of situations that require hand seam sealing: (1) if the factory-applied seam tape starts to peel (see James Dziezynski's story, right) and (2) if your tent lacks seam taping from the get-go.

This is a factory-taped seam.

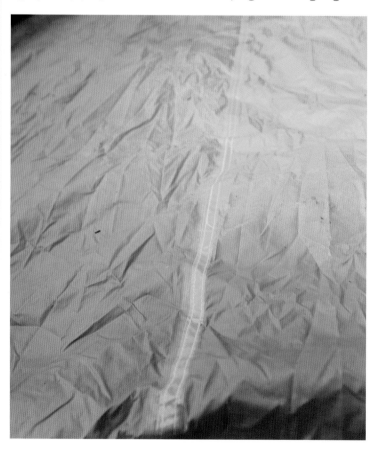

REAL PEOPLE, REAL PROBLEMS: FIXING PEELING SEAM TAPE

Boulder-based writer **James Dziezynski**, author of *Best Summit Hikes in Colorado,* has gone all over the world with his North Face Slickrock tent. After twelve years of hard use everywhere from Greenland to Antarctica, the seams finally gave up during an unexpected rain squall at Snowmass Lake in Colorado. It had been a long time coming. Between getting baked in the dry desert of Moab and frozen in the Canadian Rockies, it had been a while since heavy rain had tested the seams. The good news was he didn't have to go down to the lake to find a suitable water source; he could filter it from his sleeping bag. Literally.

Step 1: Carefully peel the old tape off completely. Scrape any little stray bits of tape off with a butter knife. Clean the seams using an alcohol prep pad and let dry.

Step 2: Next, install the applicator brush on a tube of Seam Grip. (I highly recommend using the brush for seam sealing; it makes for much quicker, neater work.) Simply paint along the seam, being sure to cover both lines of stitching. Let cure overnight.

The Fix: Start by setting up the tent and staking it down well to create a taut shape. Then follow this easy two-step process.

James Dziezynski atop Jasper Peak (12,932 feet) in Colorado.

SEAM SEALING

First, choose your poison. For double-wall tents (which have a polyurethane coating on the interior of the fly and on the floor), go with Seam Grip. For any silnylon (nylon that has been impregnated with silicone to make it waterproof) fabrics, go with SilNet, which is the only adhesive that will stick to this slippery fabric. For single-wall tents that have not been factory seam-taped, check with the manufacturer to see whether it recommends Seam Grip or SilNet.

Step 1: Apply a generous bead of sealer—enough so that it covers both stitch lines.

Step 2: Use a brush to paint the sealer over each stitch.

Set your tent up outside or in a well-ventilated area. Stake it out so that all the seams are taut. If sealing a rainfly, attach it to the tent inside out, so the interior face of the material is facing out. (You typically want to seal the underside of a double-wall tent's rainfly, where the shiny polyurethane coating is; if you're dealing with a single-wall tent, the manufacturer often suggests sealing the outside.) Apply your sealer along all exposed seams in a thin, even coat, using a small brush (an old toothbrush works fine if you don't have the applicator brush that came with the adhesive) to work the sealer into the stitch holes. Some tips:

- Pay extra attention to corners, anywhere the stake-out or guy-out loops attach to the tent body.
- Thicker is not better. Thick coats of sealer tend to peel eventually. Your best bet is to thin the sealer (for Seam Grip use Cotol-240; for SilNet use mineral spirits) so it's easy to apply and melts into the tiny stitch holes. Use 1 part Cotol-240 or mineral spirits to 3 to 4 parts Seam Grip or SilNet.
- Use a plastic syringe for tricky, tight spots.
- SilNet—even when it's dry—can stick to itself. Dust the seams with talcum powder to prevent this from happening.

SEAM GRIP TIPS

When your timeline is tight (as in, you're leaving on a trip tomorrow and just discovered that you need to make a Seam Grip repair, which typically takes at least eight hours to cure thoroughly), grab a bottle of McNett Cotol-240. On a nonporous surface, like a plastic or metal plate, mix one part Cotol-240 with three to four parts Seam Grip, using a toothpick or plastic knife to combine. Use this Seam Grip mixture for your repair as you normally would. In about two hours it'll be dry and ready to pack up!

Also, before you recap your Seam Grip, take a minute to wipe down the threads with a paper towel, and then twist the cap on tightly. I've had to pitch many a half-used tube of Seam Grip because I didn't put it away properly and the stuff solidified and choked the opening. One tube should last through many repairs if you put it away correctly. Store opened tubes of Seam Grip in the freezer (defrost before using) for maximum shelf life.

Peeling or Worn-off Coatings

The rainfly and floor of your tent are coated with a thick, tough polyurethane. If you take good care of your tent, you'll never give it a second thought, but sometimes those coatings can wear off or—worse—start to peel. This is typically caused by improper storage, UV damage, or simply old age. If you want to refresh or restore this waterproof coating, it can be laborious, but if you've got the time and patience, it may be worth it. Your call. If you're inclined, here's the drill:

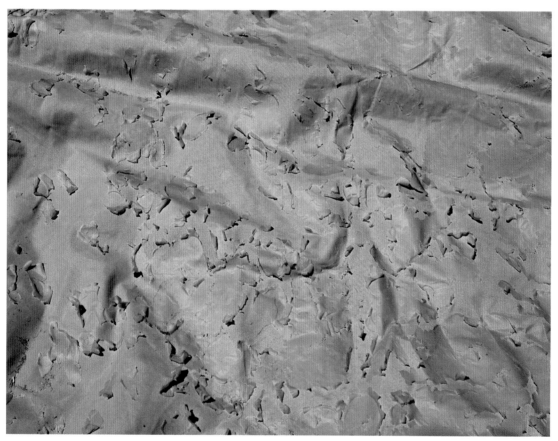

Step 1: Remove as much of the old coating as possible. If it's loose or flaky (like this one), try scrubbing with a stiff brush or (very gently) with steel wool. You can even put it through a cycle of the washing machine (this is the only time you should ever wash your tent in this fashion) to loosen the coating. Before you re-treat, make sure that there are no loose flakes. (**Note:** If the coating is at all tacky, the tent is shot, and can't be revitalized.)

Step 2: Clean the area well with water, removing any fine dust that may have resulted from all your scrubbing. Let dry thoroughly. The fabric should look smooth, consistent, and as naked as a baby's bum!

Step 3: For a tent floor, set up and stake out the tent. For a fly, spread it out flat on a very clean surface. (I suggest purchasing some new plastic sheeting from a hardware store to use as your surface. Trust me, it will make a big difference, because as the sealer soaks into the fabric, it will pick up any debris on the other side, and it's brutal, if not impossible, to get off.) Then apply a thin, even coat of Aquaseal Poly Coat (this is my favorite product, but there are others). Let dry completely, then sprinkle with talcum powder (to prevent sticking) before packing.

Removing Mildewy Smell

Reality check: Once those ugly black mildew stains appear on your tent, they're there for life. Deal with it, and don't let it happen again (see "Prevention" section)! As for that rank smell that always comes hand in hand with mildew stains? There is something you can do about that. I've had great luck with this technique:

Step 1: Fill a big plastic tub with water and about a cup of Lysol. Submerge the tent and let it soak for a few minutes. Then pull it out and rinse it off (either with a garden hose or by submerging it again in clean water). Set the tent up and let it dry.

Step 2: Mix one cup of salt, one cup of concentrated lemon juice, and one gallon of hot water. Scrub the tent down using a vegetable brush or big sponge, then let it air-dry again.

Care and Maintenance

PREVENTION

The number-one mantra when it comes to caring for your tent is this: Dry it out after every trip! Store your tent wet, even just ever-so-slightly damp, and the next time you unfurl it, it will at best smell like feet, and at worst it could be covered in mildew.

On the trail we're often forced to pack a sodden tent after a rainy night, heavy condensation, or a fresh blanket of dew. Don't sweat it, but as soon as you get to camp, set it up and let it air out. When you return home, hopefully the skies have cleared and you can pitch it in your yard for a thorough drying. If it's still raining, hang it somewhere inside and fluff it around every once in a while until it dries out.

SEASONAL CLEANING

Every spring I like to give all my tents a good scrubbing to remove the dead bug guts, spilled sunscreen, and ground-in dirt that smears the walls, floor, and fly. Pick a nice sunny day, pitch your tent in the yard, and fill a bucket with warm water and a squirt of mild dish soap (Joy or Dawn works well). Get to work with a sponge and/or plastic-bristled veggie brush and scrub 'er down, inside and out. For the rainfly, spread it out on the ground and do one side at a time. Don't forget the corners, zipper tracks, and stuff sacks, too. Then refill the bucket with fresh water and rinse everything clean. Let it all air-dry thoroughly. Don't forget the poles: When grit builds up or gets caught in the hollow sections, it can eventually abrade the tips so they don't fit together as cleanly as they should. Give each pole section a good blast with the garden hose to remove any grit, then towel them dry.

I also take this opportunity to inspect all the stakes that come with each tent, so I remember to replace lost, bent, or broken ones. And I check all the guy-out points to make sure the tent is fully rigged, so it's ready for the next big storm!

Splurge!

When you've exhausted all efforts and it's time to buy a new tent, consider these features, as well as the pros and cons of each to help you make the best purchase. Set up the ones you like in the store, crawl inside, and try to picture you, your hiking buddy, and all your gear. Is it big enough?

PICK THIS . . .	OR THAT
Freestanding: Self-supporting pole structure good for rocky, stubborn ground (but vestibules often still require stakes)	**Not freestanding:** Usually lighter and with smaller footprints that are easier to fit in tight spots, but requires stakes; terrain (sand, snow) can be a limitation
Pole sleeves: More stable in windy or rainy conditions, but slower to pitch and less air movement	**Pole clips:** Setup is fast and airflow superior, but tent can be less stable in wind
One entrance: Lighter, but less convenient—you may have to crawl over your tentmate to exit	**Two entrances:** Maximum storage space, ventilation, egress, and inclement-weather cooking space
All-mesh body: Increases ventilation; reduces weight; allows stargazing	**All-fabric body:** Captures more body heat in cold temps; blocks cold and spindrift
Dark color: Absorbs heat and blocks light for late sleepers	**Bright color:** More cheerful ambience for storm-bound days; easier to spot in rescue situations
Double wall: Separate tent body and rainfly make for better ventilation, less condensation	**Single wall:** Best for cold, dry conditions; easy to set up; weighs less, but can be stuffy and damp if conditions are warmer
Urethane: Waterproof coating. Cheaper; not as strong for its weight	**Silnylon:** Waterproof and lightweight
Aluminum poles: Less expensive; more durable; easier to repair	**Carbon fiber poles:** Super light and strong, but expensive

Other Tent Considerations

STAKE SELECTION

All tents come with stakes, of course, but that doesn't mean you have to stick with what the manufacturer has decided for you. Choose your stakes based on the terrain you'll be camping on; different designs and shapes are tailored to various types of surfaces. (*Tip:* Always pack a few extra in case you bend one in a fatal way or lose one in the dark.)

- Headed to a car campground? The plastic yellow ones (below) work well in soft, loamy soil.
- Anticipate rocky ground? Go with sturdy T-shaped aluminum ones (the T refers to a cross-section of the stake, not a side view).
- High-use areas? If the ground is compacted like cement, a screw-in stake will get the job done.
- All-purpose. These straight aluminum pins strike a good balance between durability and light weight.
- Camping on sand or snow? You want stakes with maximum surface area (like the big orange one pictured below). Or make your own "deadmen" stakes. Learn how on page 68.
- Going ultralight? Opt for pencil-skinny titanium or lightweight aluminum hook stakes.

Stakes come in an array of sizes, shapes, and materials, each designed to work in a different type of terrain and under different conditions.

STUFF OR ROLL?

This is a hotly contested topic: Should you meticulously fold and roll your tent before putting it in its stuff sack or should you stuff it like a sleeping bag? My opinion is that it's really personal preference. Me, I'm a stuffer. It's just way easier and faster. Tent company reps have told me different things: Some say that repeated creasing will eventually damage the waterproof coatings; others say that stuffing it can cause the same problem over time. Like I said, it comes down to preference.

One thing's certain, though: Make sure your tent is totally, 100 percent, completely dry before storing it for any period of time. Not to be a broken record on this topic, but it's key: Cramming a wet tent into a stuff sack and letting it sit is when the real damage happens.

THE EFFECTS OF UV

Tents can sunburn, too! Well, not really, but prolonged exposure to bright sun can damage and weaken your tent's fabrics. Don't worry about your sunny campsite on a weekend trip—that won't cause any real damage. But if you're using your tent intensively—like every day while you hike a long trail, or all summer long as the kids' playhouse in the yard—be sure to pitch it in a shady spot.

Make Ultralight Deadman Stakes

To make a "deadman," you can use just about anything you have on hand—sticks, collapsed trekking poles, even stuff sacks filled with sand or snow. The idea is to use objects that have more surface area than a puny tent stake and secure them to the stake-out loops on your tent. Then you bury these items—the deeper the better (like a dead man)—to create a strong anchor. If you frequently camp on snow or sand, consider making these ultralight deadmen and packing them with your tent. That way you won't have to scramble in camp to find other items to use. These deadmen weigh only 0.6 ounce each, so you won't begrudge carrying a few.

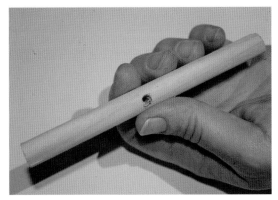

Step 1: Cut a ¾-inch wooden dowel or other non-temperature-conducting material into 6-inch-long sections. Sand the ends smooth so they don't tear tent fabric.

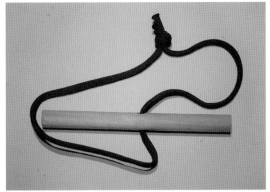

Step 2: Drill a hole through the center of the dowel and tie an 18- to 20-inch piece of nylon cord through it. This deadman, as shown, weighs a mere 0.6 ounce.

Step 3: Slip the cord end through the stake-out loops or guylines of your tent, then feed the dowel through the cord loop.

Step 4: It ends up attached like this. Repeat for all stake-out loops and guylines. The deadmen are easily added or removed when necessary.

This campsite in Iceland seemed like a good idea at the time, but when the tide came in, we had to scurry to move it about 10 feet back. Lesson learned!

Tips from the Field: Tents

- **Choosing a site:** Always opt for a previously used or established campsite whenever possible, to avoid causing unnecessary impact to the landscape. Look for elevated, well-drained sites (so you don't end up floating in a puddle should a storm hit), and try to camp at least 200 feet from any water source or trail. And look up! Don't pitch your tent below any precarious tree branches or boulder fields.

- **Prerig your tent:** Locate all the guy-out points and attach the lines before you leave. Either rig the lines with tensioners (common at outdoor shops) or learn the tautline hitch, which allows you to stake out the end and adjust the tension by sliding the knot up the line.

- **Venting:** In order to prevent condensation buildup inside your tent, you need to create some airflow. Whenever possible you want a low vent (this can often be accomplished by staking the rainfly out taut away from the bottom perimeter of the tent) so cool air can flow in and a high vent (many tents have ceiling vents built in, but you can also arrange the door so that it's open on top) so moist air can escape.

- **Don't skip the fly:** I can't tell you how many nights I've looked up and seen stars, then decided to skip the rainfly in lieu of the Milky Way views, only to have to run around like a maniac at 3 a.m. when a storm rolled in. At the very least attach the fly to one side of the tent so it's ready to quickly deploy if the rain starts. That way you're not fumbling in the dark to try to match up the corners.

- **Keep boots out:** Impose a strict "no boots in the tent" rule and make sure everyone leaves their muddy footwear in the vestibule to keep your living space as pristine as possible.

- **Improvise a vestibule:** If your tent lacks ample vestibule space for storing your pack, just pack a couple of giant, black, heavy-duty garbage bags. Before bed cozy your pack up inside and lean it upright against a rock or tree. It'll stay dry no matter what.

CHAPTER SIX

Boots

Undoubtedly one of the most important pieces of gear in our arsenal, boots have a very direct effect on the comfort and success of any hiking trip. It sometimes takes years of trial and error to find a pair of boots that you fall in love with, and when that happens, you'll do anything to keep them functioning, right?

In general, the heavier the boot, the longer it will last. If you opt for a $100 pair of super-light low-cut hikers, don't expect them to last as long as a $250 pair of full-grain leather big boys, like those pictured at left. Like I said, the lighter the shoe, the more disposable it becomes. So while most of the fixes in this chapter pertain to boots that are meant to last several years or more, many of them can also be applied to light hikers, too.

Holes

Small holes are rare in all-leather models, but they do happen in high wear points—like toe creases (see below)—on fabric boots.

Clean the area well with rubbing alcohol (use a toothbrush to remove any grit from the creases). Then bust out the Seam Grip and plug the holes with a generous gob. Let cure overnight.

PRO FIX

Hiking boots are like cars: When the odometer hits so many miles, it's time for retirement. But some things are worth fixing first.

- If the soles of your heavy-leather hikers are worn smooth, but the boot is otherwise in good shape, send them to a good cobbler for a sole replacement. I recommend Dave Page out of Seattle (davepagecobbler.com), and so do the majority of boot makers out there. Dave can resole your heavy-duty hikers or mountaineering boots for under $100.

- a lace hook pops off

- stitching blows out in a major way

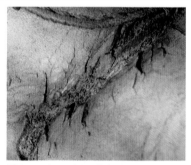

This up-close shot of the toe crease area on an all-leather boot shows some serious neglect. If leather gets to this point, it's time to go shopping.

Peeling Rands

If you spot a peeling rand, the key is to fix it up fast, before the whole sole starts to come away (see "Rebonding Soles").

Step 1: Take a screwdriver or something with a similar profile and shape and gently clean any dirt or debris from the gap between boot and rand. (This allows for better adhesion.)

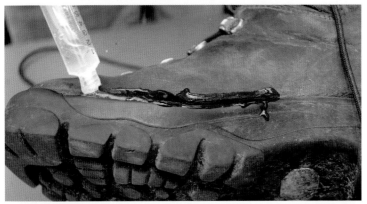

Step 2: Fill an irrigation syringe with Freesole, Shoe Goo, or Seam Grip. Squirt the adhesive into the gap.

Step 3: Tape the rand firmly in place, using a pencil to apply direct pressure to any problem spots. Let cure overnight.

Matt Vellone, of Boulder, Colorado, has traveled the world—from New Zealand to Alaska—in his eight-year-old leather Raichles. "They've taken a beating," he says. "I had them resoled a few years back, but they delaminated a year ago in the North Cascades. I've yet to find another pair of boots that fit my feet so well, so I'd love to get them back on the trail."

The Fix: If the toe of your boot starts flapping, the adhesive that joins the sole to the upper has given out. This often happens because your boots were exposed to excessive heat (see "Drying Your Boots"). If you're in the field, there's not much you can do short of wrapping it with duct tape, but once home the fix is pretty simple and will let you get many more miles out of your boot. (***Note:*** If the sole peels off cleanly like Matt's—either in the toe or heel area—and you catch it quickly, it's oh-so-simple. If you let it go for a while, or if the boot has multiple layers that get exposed once the sole has peeled, it gets slightly more complicated, but it's still fixable—see Melanie's story, right.)

Matt Vellone poses with his boots at 13,000 feet along the Continental Divide Trail in Colorado.

Step 1: Wipe both surfaces—the inside of the rubber sole and the leather—down with rubbing alcohol. Fill the sole cavity with Freesole or Shoe Goo.

Step 2: Tape or clamp the sole securely in place. Let it cure overnight, or better yet, for forty-eight hours. (***Note:*** Some adhesive will inevitably ooze out of the gap. Don't worry about it—they're hiking boots, not dress shoes!)

Melanie Robinson moved to Colorado in 2007 in search of open spaces and vertical gain. The first thing she bought when she arrived was her Asolo Stynger GTX boots. "They have hiked more miles of trail than I can count, climbed two 14ers, as well as many small peaks along the way," she says. "I literally wore them every day until the soles gradually delaminated and I started tripping over myself with each step!"

The Fix: This was a tricky one because the sole on these boots has multiple layers, all of which were exposed when the toe peeled away. This repair took a whole lot of Freesole and Seam Grip, but I eventually got this boot back in fighting shape. Here's how:

Melanie Robinson taking a breather on the summit of Mount Muscoco in Colorado.

Step 1: This boot is in a bad way. Not only has the sole peeled away, exposing the other materials in the boot, but some of the rubber has degraded away.

Step 2: Gently peel back the toe and clean out any dirt. Then liberally squirt Freesole onto both surfaces.

Step 3: Carefully marry the upper to the sole, making sure that the upper is neatly tucked inside the sole.

Step 4: To keep everything nice and tight while the adhesive cures—up to forty-eight hours—completely wrap the front of the boot with duct tape.

Restoring Worn Heels

Many people, because of their particular gait, experience undue wear in the heel area of a shoe or boot. This can be frustrating when the rest of the boot is still in great condition. But there is an easy way to restore your heels to maintain traction and keep your funky gait from getting worse. Here's the scoop:

Step 1: Apply a piece of clear tape to the perimeter of the heel to make a dam. Squirt a generous amount of Freesole into the cavity.

Step 2: Use a plastic knife to gently feather the adhesive. Then set the boots perfectly level so the goo can spread evenly. Let it cure for forty-eight hours.

Step 3: Remove the tape and you have a brand-new heel.

Making a Toe Cap

Lots of leather boots come with rubber toe rands to protect the leather from abrasion in this vulnerable spot, but many don't. If your boots fall into the latter category and your precious toes are getting scuffed, try this quick, effective solution: Build your own toe cap.

Step 1: Mark off the area you want to protect with a piece of tape.

Step 2: Lightly scuff up the toe area with sandpaper.

Step 3: Wipe your scuff job down with rubbing alcohol to remove any debris.

Step 4: Apply McNett Freesole to the top of the toe, and then use a foam brush, Popsicle stick, or even a toothpick to move the adhesive over the entire section. Don't worry about evening it out; the Freesole will self-adjust into a nice smooth sheen.

Step 5: Remove the tape after about thirty minutes, then let your boots cure overnight.

Cleaning

There's something very gratifying about giving your boots their own little spa day. You start off with dusty, dirt-encrusted clompers, and less than an hour later you have boots that look spanking new. Follow these easy steps any time your boots come home from a trip looking particularly thrashed.

Step 1: Fresh back from a grueling trip, your boots will look something like this: dusty, caked with muck, scuffed, and generally forlorn. Remove the laces (toss them in the washing machine or dishwasher), and wet the boots.

Step 2: Fill a bucket with about a half gallon of water and either a purpose-built boot cleaner like ReviveX Boot Cleaner Concentrate or a drop of mild dish soap. Scrub the boot aggressively with a medium stiff brush (a toothbrush also works). Then rinse under the faucet or with a hose. Let air-dry in the sun and proceed to waterproofing, right.

REMOVING PESKY SMELLS

Do you suffer from stinky boot syndrome? Do your tentmates gag when you remove them at the end of the day? It's probably not the boot itself, but the sweat-soaked insole. Some tips for squelching the stench:

- During a trip remove the insoles each night so they can air-dry.
- Back home wash the inside of your boot with a mild dish soap and water (or use McNett Mirazyme, an enzyme-based odor eliminator). Pay special attention to the insole. Rinse in a 3:1 hot water–to–white vinegar solution.
- Stuff the boots with newspaper and turn them upside down to dry. Change newspaper as needed, until the boots are dry.

Waterproofing

There are two kinds of boots out there: those that are water-proof and those that are not. To be truly waterproof a boot must have a membrane—like Gore-Tex—sandwiched inside the materials. Boots with membranes rarely, if ever, leak, even though many people swear that they do. They don't. What's really happening is that the boot's original DWR (durable water repellent) has worn off, so the materials—whether it's leather or fabric—get saturated. The inner membrane prevents the water from reaching your foot, but the damage is done: Your foot perceives the wetness (and coldness) outside the membrane, and it tells your brain "my foot is wet" even though it's really not. The bottom line: Keep your boots well conditioned (see "Conditioning Leather Boots") and regularly treat them with a waterproofer, and your feet will feel—and stay—dry.

How often should you waterproof your boots? It depends on how hard you use them. Any time you start to see water penetrate the material, that's your signal. For heavy users this could be up to a couple times a season.

Conditioning Leather Boots

Leather is like skin: It needs periodic moisturizing or it will begin to dry out and crack like an old snake. All boots with leather (either full or partial) should be conditioned any time they start looking parched (you'll notice the leather turning a lighter shade). Don't wait for cracks or creases to form, because once they do, there's no stopping them. There are many condition- ing products out there, but personally I prefer Aquaseal Leather Waterproofing and Conditioner (aquaseal.com) because it's a twofer: It saves me a step and does a great job at both tasks.

Whatever you do, don't use mink oil or any other straight oil to condition your boots. It oversoftens the leather and causes it to lose its structural integrity, which is key to keeping your foot supported. The only exception: If you have a big burly pair of all-leather jobs that are resisting break-in, it's okay to apply small amounts of mink oil to troublesome spots to beat the leather into submission. But use a small amount at a time and don't overdo it.

Aquaseal is a cream, and leather considers it delicious. Apply several thin coats with your fingers and your leather will drink it up.

Drying Your Boots

Back when I was a rookie backpacker, I took a fabulous week-long gear-testing trip to the Wind Rivers in Wyoming. On day one we crossed countless creeks and rivers, and my boots got alternately soaked and caked with mud. It was a cold night and had started to snow. I couldn't bear the thought of wet leather boots the next morning, so I dried them by our blazing campfire. That morning my boots were nice and dry, all right. But they had also shrunk by about half a size, which I quickly determined after about half a mile of walking. Worse still, we had many more stream crossings that day, too, so my boots were quickly soaked again.

I ended the day (and suffered throughout the rest of the trip) with huge, quarter-size blisters rubbed raw on both heels.

What I should have done was dealt with it. Sometimes wet boots are a fact of hiking in beautiful places. I should have just removed the insoles, opened up the laces, and placed the boots inside the foot of my sleeping bag that night. They would have likely still been damp the next morning, but I'll take damp over blisters any day.

Bottom line: Drying takes time. Don't force it. Keep your boots clear of intense heat, which can also damage the glues that bond the boot together and lead to delaminating.

Sometimes there's no avoiding soaked boots. The key is knowing how to dry them out properly, and patiently.

Splurge!

When you've exhausted all efforts and it's time to buy new boots, consider these features, as well as the pros and cons of each to help you make the best purchase. Also, be sure to try on as many brands as you can (with your hiking socks, not your dress socks!) to find the one that best jives with your foot shape. And check out my boot-fitting tips in "Boot Fitting 101."

PICK THIS . . .	OR THAT
Low cut: Best for light and fast hikes on smooth terrain; no break-in required	**High cut:** Better ankle protection for gnarly territory and heavy loads
Waterproof : Membranes such as Gore-Tex, eVent, or OutDry keep you bone dry—but boost the price tag	**Nonwaterproof:** Best breathability for hot, dry environs and sweaty feet
Synthetic: Man-made "leathers," polyester, and nylon materials reduce weight, are more breathable, and dry out faster when soaked (bonus: very low-maintenance)	**Leather:** Break-in time and periodic TLC required, but durable leathers reign supreme for big loads and tough terrain
Full-grain leather: Bomber durability and protection	**Split-grain leather:** Lighter, less expensive, and softer; requires less break-in time
Plastic/fabric lace hardware: Shaves a bit of weight, though it's less durable; webbing eyelets prevent laces from slipping	**Metal lace hardware:** Laces slide easily through metal eyelets and ankle speed hooks, allowing quick adjustments for ascents and descents
Synthetic liners: Wick sweat and promote breathability	**Leather liners:** Lusciously mold to feet, but trap heat and dry slowly
Soft, sticky rubber soles: Flex allows a natural stride (especially when walking quickly); tacky rubber allows better smearing when scrambling	**Hard, stiff rubber soles:** Absorb shock on hard landings, protect the bottom of feet from bruising, and last longer
Shallow lugs: Shed mud effectively	**Deep lugs:** Better grip in mud and snow

Boot Fitting 101

Blisters, blackened toenails, sprained arches, bone spurs, plantar fasciitis: need any more convincing that the proper fit is vitally important? Read on.

- Always try boots on at the end of the day, when your feet are slightly swollen, like they would be after a day of hiking.

- Wear your hiking socks, not your dress socks, which are too thin to give you an accurate idea of fit. Many new-generation hiking socks come with areas of differing thickness that can significantly alter boot fit as well.

- Ignore your preconceived notions about your foot. Our feet flatten out and expand as we age, so get your feet measured by a pro every time you buy.

- Use your true measurement as a starting point, but don't get hung up on it. If you measure a 10, also try on a 9.5 and a 10.5 to see which one feels best.

- Walk around in your chosen candidates. You should feel little to no movement in the heel area. The boot should be snug through the midfoot and you should have plenty of toe-wiggling room.

- Kick your toe against a wall or column. The toes should barely graze (if at all) the front of the boot. If they do, that could spell trouble on a long descent.

- Consider upgrading insoles. Most boots come with flimsy footbeds that don't offer much support. Aftermarket insoles (Superfeet and Sole are two of my favorite brands) provide much-needed arch support and a smooth heel pocket and can greatly improve the fit of your boot, especially if you have low-volume, narrow feet.

- For truly persistent problems you might need custom-molded orthotics. These rigid and often expensive ($150 and up) footbeds must be fitted by a podiatrist. To determine whether you might need orthotics, look at the wear patterns on the soles of your older shoes and boots. If they show extreme

FRAYING BOOT LACES?

Solve this annoying little problem in a matter of seconds. Just use your multitool to snip the laces below the fray, then char the ends to prevent further unraveling.

wear on the inner side of the soles (pronation) or the outer side (supination), then your ankles and arches probably need orthotic support.

Tips from the Field: Boots

- **Pack camp shoes:** Especially if you're hiking in heavy, stiff boots, it's a sweet luxury to slip into something more comfortable at the end of a 10-mile day. Consider down booties in cold weather, or flip-flops or Crocs in mild weather.

- **Nip blisters in the bud:** Don't wait for a big gaping blister to form. As soon as you begin to feel a hot spot, stop, inspect your feet, and do something about it. Changing socks can help, and you can also apply duct or medical tape to the hot spot to prevent more friction.

- **Relace your boots:** Experiment with different lacing techniques (you'll find lots of info at backpacker.com) to relieve pressure points at the tops of your feet or to better lock your heel into the boot's pocket to prevent movement. Remember: Movement creates friction and friction leads to blisters.

- **Boots leaking?** If you're on a trip and wishing you had forked over the extra dough for waterproof boots, there is a solution, albeit an imperfect one. Place a plastic bag (a large zip-top bag, a grocery bag, or even a cut-up black garbage bag) over each sock, then lace up your boots. The plastic will keep out the water, but your feet will get hot.

Don't be afraid of a little mud. According to Leave No Trace principles (see Chapter 14), it's always better to carefully make your way through a puddle than skirt around it and widen the trail.

CHAPTER SEVEN

Sleeping Bags

Tears and Holes

Most sleeping bag shell fabrics are pretty wispy (designers use this fabric because it's lightweight and very breathable, so the bag won't trap your body heat in the form of condensation), so chances are, if you use your bag long enough, it will probably sustain some kind of wound, be it a clean tear or a burn hole from a candle lantern. The fix is easy and (thankfully) sew-free, assuming that the wound isn't gigantic (in which case the tape won't cover it). This fix works for all sleeping bags—down and synthetic—as well as any insulated clothing and can be done right in the field at the scene of the crime.

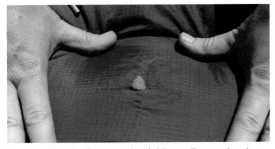

My son's sleeping bag sustained this small tear when he was dragging it around our camp in New Hampshire's White Mountains.

Step 1: Clean the area with an alcohol prep pad.

Step 2: Cut a rounded patch of Tear-Aid that covers the problem spot by at least ½ inch on every side.

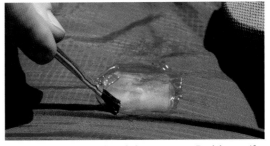

Step 3: Apply the patch with firm pressure. Back home, if you have the desire to reinforce the patch, just paint the circumference with Seam Grip.

FIXING TINY HOLES

Check out the quick fix for tiny holes in Chapter 2. It works like a charm for sleeping bags, too.

Care and Maintenance

The key to keeping your sleeping bag working properly is maintaining its "loft." Loft refers to the thickness of the bag, and it's directly connected to a bag's ability to trap the warmth created by your body. You can keep your bag as lofty as the day you bought it as long as you do two things: store it properly and wash it properly.

FIELD TIP

Over the course of a trip, a sleeping bag can gain water weight (and lose loft) because your body sweats at night, and that sweat migrates into the insulation. It's good practice to pull your bag out of the tent first thing in the morning and sling it over a branch or the tent to let it air-dry while you make breakfast and break camp.

Each morning give your bag a little time in the sun (provided the weather is cooperating).

STORING YOUR BAG

Most good bags these days come with two sacks: a small one intended for short-term use on the trail and a large, cotton or mesh one that's intended for long-term storage. It may be tempting to save closet space and keep your bag neatly packed in its tiny sack. Don't do it. Many good bags have been permanently crippled in this fashion. Whether it's down- or synthetic-filled, keeping your bag compressed like that for long periods of time will do permanent damage to the insulation and prevent it from rebounding into its lofty glory.

If your bag is older and didn't come with a storage sack (or if you lost it), opt for a king-size cotton pillowcase (cinched closed with a rubber band). Other options: Hang it in a closet or store it flat under your bed. It doesn't matter which method

REPLACING WORN SLIDERS

For step-by-step instructions, check out Chapter 3.

Left to right: A king-size pillowcase makes a great makeshift bag sack; a standard mesh storage sack; a compressed bag is ideal for on-trail storage.

you choose, as long as the bag is allowed to breathe and rest in its fluffiest form in an environment that's cool and dry. In other words, if your basement or garage tends toward the damp, mildewy side, don't store your bag (or any of your other gear, for that matter) there.

WASHING YOUR BAG

How often should you clean your bag? Any time you start to notice a decrease in the loft or a gross odor. This generally happens after twenty to thirty nights of use. (If you opt to use a sleeping bag liner—made of polyester or silk—you won't need to wash your bag as often, because the liner will catch your body oils, sunscreen, and bug repellent and prevent them from migrating into your bag.)

First rule: Don't dry-clean it. Dry-cleaners use powerful solvents that strip down feathers of their natural oils and coat synthetic fibers so that they can't breathe.

Second rule: Don't wash your bag at home, for two reasons: (1) Many home washers have center agitators, which can damage the bag and (2) you need a giant, commercial-size washer (and dryer) to do the job right. Load your pockets with quarters and head to the Laundromat.

Spot cleaning

If your bag has a beef stew stain on the shell, but is otherwise clean and fluffy, or if you want to pretreat a stained area before you throw it in the wash, just mix a little powdered laundry soap and water into a paste. Then hold the shell fabric away from the insulation (to keep it from getting wet) and scrub the stain using an old toothbrush. Rinse and let air-dry.

Choose a soap

Most bag-makers recommend specific, purpose-built soaps for washing sleeping bags, like Nikwax Down Wash or Tech Wash (for synthetic insulated bags) (nikwax.com). The reason?

Typical laundry soaps and detergents leave behind residue that can inhibit the performance of your gear, either by squelching its loft, hampering its DWR (durable water repellent), or clogging pores to restrict breathability. Bottom line: A special, purpose-built soap is worth the investment.

READY TO WASH

When you're at the Laundromat and ready to wash, follow these steps:

1. If your bag has a waterproof shell, turn it inside out. This allows the water and soap to flow freely through the insulation and materials. Zip it up and fasten any Velcro closures.

2. Put it in that big old washer and set it for warm water on the delicate cycle.

3. When the cycle is complete, run it through an additional rinse-and-spin cycle to remove any extra soap and water.

4. Remove the bag from the washer (don't be alarmed by its flat, sodden appearance) and lay it out on a folding table. Give the outer shell a quick spray with a water repellent, such as ReviveX Spray-On Water Repellent for Outerwear (mcnett.com). This will give the fabric some added water resistance.

5. Place the bag in a giant dryer, set it to low, and start plugging in quarters. (**Note:** Some people recommend adding tennis balls [for down bags] to break up clumps. But this really isn't necessary. The tumbling action of the dryer will do the job, and you can manually break up any visible clumps between cycles. Be patient: It will take up to a few hours.)

6. Back home, unzip the bag and let it air-dry overnight.

PRO FIX

For these big repairs, send your bag back to the manufacturer for best results.

- A full zipper replacement
- Torn interior baffles (when all the down has shifted to one spot; the bag might be shot, but it might also be covered under warranty)
- Needs more down added

This down bag was in rough shape after sustaining a bad rip. But the owner sent it back to the manufacturer, Feathered Friends, which promptly restuffed it and sewed it back up.

REAL PEOPLE, REAL PROBLEMS:
RIPPED-OUT DRAWCORD

Abby Baur inherited a big red sleeping bag from her uncle. It's a good-quality (albeit heavy) down bag by Eddie Bauer. Abby adores the bag for sentimental reasons but also loves to use it for car-camping trips in her home state of Alaska. "This bag is at least thirty-five years old," she says. "And as gross as it sounds, it may have never been washed. It's kind of deflated and smelly, plus the drawcord around the hood enclosure has been partially ripped out and some of the fabric around the drawcord opening has torn."

The Fix: Follow the steps shown in these photos.

Abby Baur shows off her freshly repaired bag near Kluane Lake in the Yukon.

Step 1: I cut a small slit in the drawcord channel near the base. Then I pulled the cord free of the sleeve, leaving it attached at one end to the bag. (**Note:** I cut most of it off, but left enough so that I could tie it to the new drawcord [see step 3] and pull it back through the sleeve. I thought this was rather brilliant because it meant that I didn't have to sew the new drawcord in place!)

Step 2: I attached one end of the new drawcord to a length of thin wire, then fed it through the slit and completely through to the other end.

Step 3: I tied the old ribbon (black) to the new drawcord and then pulled the new drawcord gently so that the knot disappeared into the fabric drawcord channel.

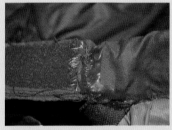

Step 4: I sewed up the slit and added a dab of Seam Grip to prevent anything from fraying or coming loose.

Step 5: The top cord was more challenging because it needed to be sewn into the bag. In other words, it needed an anchor. I decided to anchor it to the Velcro closure patch, so I made a small slit in the fabric and slid the end of the drawcord under the Velcro patch.

Step 6: I hand-sewed the living daylights out of it, going back and forth over the cord to make sure I got it firmly attached to the bag. I fed the top cord through the fabric channel (as described in step 2), then stitched up my slit and sealed it with Seam Grip.

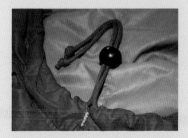

Step 7: With the two cords in place, I joined them using a cord lock and sewed up the fraying fabric around the channels.

Splurge!

Standing in an outdoor shop before a bewildering wall of bags, all of which look warm and cozy, how the heck do you choose? Don't pick your favorite color. Use the tables below to determine the right type of bag for you. Adjust the temperature rating up or down if you're a very cold or warm sleeper. Women and smaller-framed men should consider women's bags, which are tailored for slighter builds and have insulation distributed differently, but don't get hung up on gender labels. Men can use women's bags and women can use men's bags with equal success. Be sure to climb inside your chosen candidates to get a sense of the interior volume, which can vary considerably from brand to brand and model to model. Look for a fit that's roomy enough to be comfortable, yet not so voluminous that you sacrifice thermal efficiency.

FOR THIS CONDITION	CHOOSE THIS TEMPERATURE RATING	LOOK FOR THESE FEATURES
Summer, Desert	40 degrees F	Brushed or fleece lining for no-stick comfort; minimal features (hood and draft collar optional); wraparound zipper to open for blanket use
Rainforest, Wet conditions, Paddling trips	Dependent on season	Synthetic fill; water-resistant shell
Winter	0 degrees F	Adjustable draft collar; contoured hood; 6 inches of extra length for storing water bottles, clothes, and cold-sensitive gear
High mountain, Arctic	−20 degrees F or lower dependent on season	Down fill for compressibility; extra length for water-bottle and gear storage; extra girth (optional) for layering
Snow cave, Tentless	– –	Water-resistant/windproof shell or bivy sack

FOR THIS SLEEP STYLE	LOOK FOR THESE FEATURES
Thrasher	Elastic seams (for stretch); semirectangular shape or big-guy girth (for more space); or expansion panels (for adjustable space)
Snuggler	Mating zippers on same-length bags so you can cozy up with a significant other
Perspirer	Brushed or fleece lining (or bag liner); synthetic fill; breathable shell (no laminates or special coatings); two-way full-length zipper for maximum venting
Catatonic	Mummy shape for maximum thermal efficiency (and pack weight savings)

Understanding Hang Tags

All sleeping bags have a temperature rating. Some are simply generated by the bag company's design team, based on their own testing and best guesses, but more and more bag-makers are subscribing to EN ratings. EN ratings come from a standardized test called European Norm 13537. The test—an expensive procedure conducted by contracted independent labs equipped with a special heat-sensored mannequin—is designed to help consumers accurately compare ratings from manufacturer, to manufacturer. Once commissioned by the manufacturer, a lab conducts a series of tests to certify a bag's temperature rating, generating numbers that will supposedly result in you getting a warm night's sleep. If a bag has been EN-rated, you'll see three numbers on the hang tag (ratings assume that the sleeper is wearing one synthetic baselayer—top and bottom—and a hat, and using a closed-cell foam sleeping pad).

- Comfort: The lowest air temperature at which an average woman can sleep comfortably.
- Lower limit: The lowest air temperature at which an average man can sleep comfortably.
- Extreme: Survival-only rating for an average adult woman.

Bottom line: EN ratings are a strong step forward in terms of customer education, but until the entire bag industry subscribes to them, they're not the panacea that some companies had hoped for.

Tips from the Field: Sleeping Bags

- **Let it breathe:** As soon as you hit camp and set up your tent, release your bag from its stuff sack so it can have plenty of lofting time.

- **Invest in a waterproof sack:** If there's one thing that needs to stay dry, it's your sleeping bag. Buy a good sack and never again worry about a sodden bed.

- **Stuff smart:** When restuffing your bag into its sack, always start with the foot end. This allows air to escape from the bag's opening as you stuff, so it won't feel like such a wrestling match.

- **Make a pillow:** Use your bag's stuff sack as a pillowcase. Insert any extra clothes or a puffy jacket. Wrap it in a fleecy layer for extra coziness.

- **Honeymooning?** Many bags can mate together if one has a right-hand zip and the other has a left-hand zip. This is also a great option if you have an infant—just put the baby in the middle. No, you won't roll over on him or her! My kids are living proof.

- **Battling condensation?** If your tent is dripping with condensation, lay your raingear over the top of your bag to protect it from getting damp.

On cold nights in camp, don't let the warmth of your bag go to waste! Haul it out of your tent and crawl inside, and buy yourself a few more stories around the campfire.

CHAPTER EIGHT

Sleeping Pads

I remember my first sleeping pad—a thin, closed-cell foam pad that cost only 15 bucks. It did the job when I was young and foolish, but then someone lent me a standard Therm-a-Rest. The difference was pretty profound. That was twenty years ago, and sleeping pads have come a long way since then. I now sleep on supremely cushioned air mats (with insulation in cold weather), and I'll never go back. In my opinion, a comfy pad is one of the most critical pieces of gear on any trip.

Air Mattresses

One of the best gear investments you can make, an air mat can also lead to utter frustration if it springs a leak in the field. This section will teach you how to cope.

FINDING HOLES

Sometimes the leak is apparent. Sometimes it's not. If you can't find the source of the escaping air, try this: Fully inflate the pad. Then find a puddle, creek, or some other body of clear water (the stiller the better; a roiling river makes it tough to

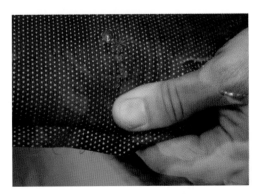

Follow the trail of bubbles to find itty-bitty pinhole leaks.

Mark the spot immediately so you don't forget where it is.

spot the problem). Submerge one end of the pad and fold it over to increase pressure. Carefully inspect the submerged portion. You're looking for tiny bubbles that will lead you to the leak. Work your way down the pad methodically, submerging and refolding each section until you spot it. Have a pen or piece of duct tape handy. When you spot the leak, you'll want to mark it clearly so that you don't have to perform this step again. Once you've marked the spot, set the pad out to dry before proceeding.

Especially if you use your pad as a camp chair, treat it carefully to prevent abrasion and holes.

REAL PEOPLE, REAL PROBLEMS: PINHOLE IN MATTRESS

Max Katzmartsic, from St. Helena, California, has a good war story about his Therm-a-Rest pad. "We had rented a houseboat on Lake Berryessa for my buddy's bachelor party. But the party lasted longer than me, so I left my friends on the boat and found a quiet spot on the little island where we were anchored. The star thistle was everywhere, unavoidable. Come morning, I had a deflated pad to go along with my headache."

The Fix: After I located the tiny pinhole by submerging it in my pool (a bathtub or mellow creek also works), I marked the spot, let the pad dry, and cleaned the area with an alcohol prep pad. Then I

Max Katzmartsic posing for a self-portrait on top of Half Dome in Yosemite.

opened the valve (this is important because you want to release the pressure inside the pad so it doesn't force the adhesive to bubble), squirted a dollop of Seam Grip over the hole, and let it dry overnight.

FIXING LARGER HOLES OR TEARS

Murphy's Law states that most pad problems happen in the middle of a backcountry trip, so the fix needs to happen fast and out there. Here's how to handle it: When you rise and shine after a grueling night of sleeping on your flat pad, get to work while everyone else has breakfast. You need to accelerate the curing process so you can sleep on your pad that night. Follow these steps:

This little tear can spell big trouble if you don't know the fix.

Step 1: Have a round adhesive patch at the ready (either Tenacious Tape or Tear-Aid). Remove the backer and mix a dollop of Seam Grip and a few drops of water using the backer as a palette (the water will speed cure time).

Step 2: Apply the mixture to the hole.

Step 3: Apply the patch with firm pressure.

Step 4: Weight it down with the heaviest rock you can find and go hiking for the day. When you come back, it should be good to go!

Washing Your Pad

You could go years and years without washing your pad, but why not give it a bath every season when you're already washing your tent or pack? It's super easy. Just inflate the pad and scrub it down with a brush and soapy water. Then let it dry. If nothing else, it will smell better.

Preventing Slippage

Sometimes the nylon shell of your sleeping bag and the nylon shell of your pad are like butter on a pancake griddle. If you've ever had that unsettling feeling of constantly slipping off your pad at night when you're camped on sloping or less-than-flat tent sites, try this simple trick to add a little friction to your pad: Add small dots of Seam Grip (or you can use silicone caulking from the home improvement store) to the pad's surface. Once it dries, the adhesive acts kind of like a boot sole—giving your pad some traction when it meets the slick nylon of your sleeping bag shell. If your pad tends to slip around on your tent floor, you can also apply some dots to the pad's underside.

No need to cover the entire pad with dots—just focus on the key points of contact: the head, shoulders, and hips.

Storing Your Pad

Uninsulated air mats can be stored rolled into their little stuff sacks. Just be sure to leave the valve open to allow any built-up moisture (from your breath) to escape. If your pad is insulated, store it flat or folded in half with the valve open—under a bed or behind a sofa works great. This is particularly important with pads that have open-cell foam inside (like standard Therm-a-Rest pads). By keeping the foam inflated, you're preserving its integrity over the long haul. Open-cell foam has a memory: If its regular state of rest is in its expanded state, it will bounce back more easily when it comes time to inflate it in the field.

Splurge!

When you've exhausted all efforts and it's time to buy a new pad, consider these features, as well as the pros and cons of each to help you make the best purchase.

TYPE	PROS	CONS
Self-inflating: Open-cell foam sandwiched between nylon	Puffs up (almost completely) by itself; foam adds insulation	Heavy; must be stored flat; sometimes requires field repairs; can be pricey
Air mat: Nylon-encased air chambers	Super light and packable; most cushion for the least weight and bulk	Patience and strong lungs needed to inflate; sometimes requires field repairs; not for cold-weather use
Insulated air mat: Nylon-encased air chambers with added down or synthetic insulation	Comfortable; warm; packable	Expensive
Closed-cell foam: Thin, dense sheet of basic foam	Cheapest, toughest, and lightest; never deflates	No inflation, so it provides the bare minimum of cushion

Tips from the Field: Sleeping Pads

- **Double up in winter:** In deep cold, you need extra insulation underneath. Get a cheap closed-cell foam pad (it has great insulative properties) and layer it under your air mattress to prevent cold from seeping through.

- **Ground check:** Before unfurling your pad, do a quick check of the ground to make sure it's smooth and free of anything that could cause a puncture.

- **Pack it inside:** Always store your air mattress inside your pack, where it's protected from abrasion.

- **Easy inflating:** Some air mattresses will tax your lungs (especially when you're at altitude). Consider investing in a little hand pump. You attach it to the valve and compress over and over to inflate your pad. Some pads come with integrated pumps.

- **Deflating:** Open the valve and start rolling from the opposite end, using your knees to compress the pad with each new roll. When you reach the end, close the valve and fold the pad in half lengthwise. Then reopen the valve and roll it toward the valve again, squeezing out the last remnants of air. Close the valve and store the pad in your pack.

REPURPOSE OLD CLOSED-CELL FOAM

Even if you've graduated from a closed-cell foam pad to a plusher one, there are lots of useful things you can do with your old pad.

· If you camp in winter, save it intact and use it underneath your air mat for added insulation.

· If you're tired of your dog pushing you off your pad, cut out a pooch-size portion and give him his own bed.

· Cut a small, butt-size square to use as a sit pad. I've used mine hundreds of times—during lunch breaks on ski trips or high in the mountains, at football games, or sitting around camp at night. Or cut it to fit the inside of your pack bag; you can pull it out to use as a butt pad, and it will give you additional protection and cushion when wearing the pack (great for ultralight frameless packs).

· Turn your regular water bottle into a thermos for tea or soup—sweet for winter trips.

· Cut a small square and cover it in duct tape. Use it as a lightweight cutting board or a stove platform on winter trips—it will prevent your stove from sinking into the snow.

Perfect for preparing your feast!

Custom-cut and tape the old foam around your favorite bottle. Add a circular top and bottom piece, using duct tape, and make a hinge for the top circle.

CHAPTER NINE

Cookware

When it comes to your camping kitchen gear, it's all about buying smart and taking good care of your investments. I've never seen or heard of catastrophic pot failure of any sort, so you really don't need to worry about repairs. For that reason, this chapter will focus on caring for your kitchenware, as well as a few tips on buying the stuff that's best suited to your needs.

Choosing Your Weapon

You can spend as little as 15 bucks on an aluminum Boy Scout mess kit or you can drop hundreds on nonstick-coated titanium pots and pans—and there are dozens of options in between. Use this table to help identify the best type for you.

TYPE	IDEAL USER	PROS	CONS
Aluminum	Thrifty shoppers	Extremely affordable	Prone to denting and sticking
Stainless steel	People who are hard on gear, use it frequently, and want it to last	Extremely durable	Heavy and prone to sticking
Nonstick-coated aluminum	Gourmet backpackers	Light and great nonstick performance	Needs TLC; nonstick coating prone to wear and scratching
Hard anodized aluminum	Typical backpackers who want a good balance of weight, performance, durability, and price	Light, fairly nonstick, easy to clean, and affordable	Slightly less nonstick than coatings
Titanium	Ultralight freaks who only need to boil water	Extremely lightweight	Expensive and prone to sticking
Nonstick-coated titanium	Ultralight freaks who also cook food	Extremely lightweight and nonstick	Very expensive; nonstick prone to wear and scratching

Caring for Your Pots and Pans

PACKING

Unless you opt for stainless cookware (which is practically immune to dents and dings), take care when packing your cookset into your backpack. Don't lash it onto the outside or pack it near the outer edges of the pack's confines. Why? Because if you're like me, you often drop your hefty pack with a thump at rest breaks and use it like a chair. If your cookware is nestled safely in the inner sanctum, surrounded by clothing, sleeping bag, and other padding, it's far less likely to dent or fall out-of-round.

It's always wise to use the space inside your pot as storage. Not only does it economize on space, but packing the pot full supports the sides of the vessel and can help prevent dents and bends. I often pack my stove, cup, bowl, and eating utensils inside, along with a little sponge and a small bottle of dish soap. Sometimes, if I'm packing in fresh vegetables or crackers, I'll use that protected space to store those items and prevent them from bruising and breaking.

Don't waste that space! The inside of a cook pot is a great place to store your kitchen stuff.

Another tip: If you use pots with nonstick coatings, a little extra care is required. Don't pack any sharp items inside the pots, as they can scrape off the coating. Place stoves in little stuff sacks and layer a sheet of fabric between the nesting pots (I use a square of absorbent polyester pack towel, which also doubles as a dishcloth).

Protect your pots from scratching in transit with a piece of fabric layered between them.

CLEANING

Ah, dish duty. If given the choice between cooking and doing the dishes, I'll choose cooking every time. But that's just me. Luckily, lots of my trip partners gladly step up to the basin at the end of the meal.

It's an important chore, too. Not only is it hygienically incorrect (and just plain gross) not to give your cooking pots a decent wash after the last bite of chili-mac is consumed, it's important that you do it correctly to preserve the life of your pots.

If your cookware is uncoated stainless or aluminum, you have no worries. Food will certainly get crusted on the surface, and you can scrape it off with metal utensils and scrub away with steel wool—all with no ill effects.

But if your pots have a nonstick coating, you've got to go easy. Here's the right way to do it:

Step 1: You've just finished eating, and the dishes need doing. Get your soap and wash rag ready. Use a camping-friendly, biodegradable soap, such as McNett Smart Suds, shown here.

Step 2: Begin by choosing your largest pot and filling it with water or, in the winter, snow.

Step 3: Heat the water over your stove until boiling. If you're melting snow, add a little water to the bottom to prevent the pan from scorching and to help it melt faster.

Step 4: Split the heated water between two pans and add a small amount of soap to one of the pans. Let the water cool enough that it won't burn you.

Step 5: Wash each dish with the rag in the soapy water and then dip it in the second pan to rinse.

Step 6: Strain out any food particles and carry them out in your trash bag. Scatter the used water at least 200 feet away from streams or other water sources.

Step 7: Voila! Clean dishes drying in the sun.

A LITTLE HELP FROM NATURE

If you forgot the sponge, look around you. There are lots of items about that make perfectly fine scrubbing implements: a pinecone, horsetail (my favorite), sand, and snow.

But don't wash your dishes directly in a pond or creek: Human food and soap residue don't do the fish any favors. Don't dump leftovers behind a stump either. Pack out what you can't eat, and if there are food remnants in your dishwater, strain them out and add them to your trash bag.

Horsetail is almost too pretty to be used as a pot scrubber, but it works great. It's found in many parts of the United States, usually near water in wet, sandy, or clay-like soil.

Caring for Your Knife

Gooey peanut butter, greasy salami, ripe cheese, campfire tinder. These are just some of the items that your pocketknife faces, so it's bound to get gunked up and dull.

A sharp knife is a good friend.

CLEANING

Knives are pretty tough. Wash 'em with soap and water and toss them in the dishwasher when you're back home. Dry them well before storing to ensure no rust creeps in. And check all the tools. Do they fold in and out smoothly? If not, add a dab of cooking oil to the hinges and you'll be back in business.

SHARPENING

A dull knife is a dangerous knife, so keep yours in good shape with periodic sharpening. There are several different methods.

Straight-edge knives

You've got two options when it comes to straight edges: either a honing stone or flat file (which requires a bit of technique) or a no-brainer guided sharpener (below right).

Honing stones and files (below left) are actually quite easy to use. Simply hold the knife's blade at an angle that matches the beveling of the blade (for most knives it's 20 degrees). Stroke the blade lightly down the stone, moving away from your body. Don't apply pressure—the weight of the blade is enough, and lighter strokes produce a finer edge. Make an equal number of strokes on each side of the blade.

For best results, some whetstones and files need to be lubricated either with oil or water; others should be used dry. Check with the manufacturer of your tool.

So easy, it's practically cheating. Just pull the knife along the fingers. Don't try this with serrated knives, only smooth blades.

Guided knife sharpeners come in many forms, but the idea is that the position of the file(s) eliminates user error in terms of angle. Simply lay the blade in the guide and pull back gently, repeating the movement until the blade is sharp.

Serrated-edge knives

Serrated or partially serrated knives can be easily sharpened, provided you have the right tool and a bit of patience, as you have to work on each serration individually. Serrated sharpeners look almost like chopsticks with handles. The filing surface is rounded and tapered, with a skinny tip (for tiny serrations) that gets thicker up toward the handle (for larger serrations). Just hold the knife against a flat surface, with the serrations tilted up. Hold the tool parallel to the work surface and place it into the gullet (the valley in between the teeth) of the first serration. Use short (½-inch) back-and-forth strokes and rotate the file as you stroke. Ten or so strokes on each gullet should do the trick. Move down through the gullets, sharpening each one equally, and positioning the tool so that the diameter of the filing surface matches each gullet.

Don't worry about sharpening the tips of a serrated blade's teeth; it's all about the sharpness of the gullet.

Dutch Ovens

I prize my big old twelve-quart dutch oven for campfire cooking. It weighs about as much as my fully loaded weekend pack, but for car camping with a big crowd, nothing beats it. I've made roasts, lasagna, cakes, crumbles, pizzas, biscuits, and stews. A good dutch oven is an heirloom. If you take proper care of it, you'll be passing it down for generations to come.

Some dutch ovens come preseasoned, which is great, and means you can start cooking in them immediately. But seasoning is an ongoing process: Do it a couple times a year to keep your oven forever young. Here's how to do it:

1. Wash your oven in hot, soapy water. (**Note:** Unless you've got serious grease to contend with, this is the only time you'll want use soap on your dutch oven. After this initial washing, it's all about hot water and elbow grease, because soap washes off the seasoning.)

Dutch ovens are all about campfire cooking, cowboy-style. Build a nice hot bed of coals, place the dutch oven on top—get the type with little legs—and layer hot coals on the flat lid to create even, all-around heat.

2. Rinse and dry it completely.

3. Using a paper towel as your applicator, rub a thin, even coating of melted shortening (like Crisco) all around the inside and outside of the oven. Don't forget the lid.

4. Preheat your home oven to 350 degrees. Place your dutch oven upside down on the top rack and the lid beside it. On the bottom rack place a baking sheet lined with aluminum foil to catch the drippings. Bake for one hour, then turn the oven off and let your dutch oven rest inside until it's completely cool.

More dutch oven tips:

- Never put it in the dishwasher.
- While on a trip, always wash it immediately after use, when the cast iron is still hot. Just use very hot water and a stiff scrubbing brush or a steel wool pad. If it's still greasy, use an SOS pad (with its embedded soap), but be sure to reseason immediately.
- After washing, dry it thoroughly and give it a light spray with vegetable oil (like Pam). Then wipe it with a paper towel and store it with the lid off (so air can circulate).

Utensils

True gear wonks love their sporks. (Some call them foons, but the gist is the same: a combination of a fork and spoon so you can twirl your spaghetti and shovel your oatmeal with the same tool.) But whether you choose a spork, a foon, traditional cutlery, or chopsticks, you'll need to pick your material:

- Titanium: ultralight
- Stainless steel: ultrastrong
- Plastic: ultracheap
- Bamboo: ultrahip

Eating utensils come in a rainbow of materials, each with its own pros and cons.

CHAPTER TEN

Stoves

Stoves are probably the most mechanical item a backpacker carries, which is why tinkering with them is so much fun (for me at least!). The two most common types of camp stoves are liquid-fuel and canister stoves; this chapter covers the most prevalent problems and fixes with both types. However, because the first step in working with stoves is diagnosing the problem based on the stove's symptoms, the chapter is organized by symptom.

Choose Your Weapon

Though backpacking stoves generally fall into the two main categories of liquid-fuel and canister, there are several subvarieties to choose from, depending on your needs. Learn the pros and cons of each before deciding.

- **White-gas stoves:** Run on the purest, most refined fuel (also called naphtha). White gas (often sold in gallon jugs) burns cleaner and hotter than other liquid fuels, and is widely

The MSR WhisperLite Internationale is one of the best, and most popular, liquid-fuel stoves on the market.

This little Optimus CruxLite canister stove weighs less than three ounces and packs down to fit in the palm of your hand.

available in the United States. In a pinch these stoves will also burn gasoline straight from the pump (manufacturers don't recommend it, and frequent cleaning is required).

- **Multi-fuel stoves:** These come with interchangeable jets that burn not only white gas, but also kerosene, jet fuel, or even diesel (great if you're traveling abroad, where white gas isn't always available). Burn white gas whenever possible—other fuels have slower boil times and require more maintenance to clear soot buildup.

- **Sit-on-top canister stoves:** These are the smallest, lightest, and most packable of all cookers because the tiny burner heads screw directly onto the threaded neck of the canister. Drawback: the higher the burner, the less stable your pot of boiling water, especially on tippy ground.

- **Remote canister stoves:** With flexible fuel lines that connect burner to canister, remote canister stoves allow the burner to sit low and squat on the ground for better big-pot stability. It also allows you to invert the canister, which can boost performance as the canister runs low. Drawback: slightly heavier and bulkier.

This Optimus stove has wide pot supports, so it's ideal for big pots.

- **Integrated systems:** These systems—in which the stove burner and pot are sold together—are ideal for people who thrive on convenience and fast boil times. They pack neatly into themselves, and boast excellent boil times and fuel efficiency. That's because when a burner and cooking pot are perfectly compatible, no fuel is wasted creating heat that skids off the side of the pot. Integrated systems also use heat exchangers—corrugated metal rings that capture and circulate heat to further boost efficiency.

- **Hybrid stoves:** Several companies make stoves that will run on virtually any fuel—canisters or any type of liquid fuel. This type of stove is expensive and a bit heavier than ideal, but if you need maximum versatility, it's a worthy trade-off.

The Jetboil Sol-Ti is an integrated canister stove system. The burner attaches to the pot/cup with a built-in heat exchanger that boosts efficiency.

For the ultimate in versatility, opt for a stove, like this MSR WhisperLite Universal, that can run on virtually any liquid-fuel or pressurized canisters.

Liquid-Fuel Stoves

These workhorse cookers are ideal for cold-weather expeditions and adventuring in developing countries. Unlike canister stoves, which suffer in cold temperatures, they perform in virtually any weather conditions. Why? Because when air pressure drops with the temperature, a liquid-fuel stove lets you pump up the bottle to compensate, while a sealed fuel canister cannot adjust. The same principle explains why liquid-fuel stoves perform better with nearly empty fuel bottles—you can add more pressure to make up for lower volume. And because fuel is stored in metal, screw-top bottles, you can pack the precise amount you need, without having to lug around empty canisters. (Canisters can also be difficult to find in remote areas and abroad.)

Liquid-fuel stoves use a pump mechanism to maintain constant pressure and steady heat output.

McGyver types also love them because they're repairable and cleanable in the field. (**Note:** There are so many different liquid-fuel stove models, and each comes with a detailed owner's manual. It's really key to read and understand the manual and identify your stove's parts, so you can work with your particular stove. I've identified some general problems and used the ubiquitous MSR WhisperLite Internationale stove to illustrate the most common problems and fixes, but like I said, these techniques will vary a bit, depending on your brand.)

WILD, ERRATIC, YELLOW FLAME

Commonplace with liquid-fuel stoves, this type of flame happens when there's a clog in either the jet (a tiny metal piece inside with a small hole that transforms the liquid fuel into a fine burnable mist) or the fuel line. It helps to start by understanding why they clog in the first place. When fuel burns, lighter, smaller molecules vaporize before the heavier ones. These heavy molecules can get left behind and turn into black carbon deposits that clog the jet or fuel line. When there's a clog, the gas can't properly vaporize, so the flame it creates is big, yellow, and potentially dangerous (if it catches on something nearby). What you want is a nice hot, concise blue flame.

This type of flame means that your stove is clogged.

Clogged jets

Many modern stoves (check your owner's manual) come with a built-in cleaning needle. If yours does, follow the instructions—it often just entails turning the stove upside down and giving it a few shakes to encourage the needle to poke through the jet and push out any debris. If your stove doesn't have this feature, or if it's not working, disassemble the jet (check your manual; it usually just means unscrewing a few pieces), soak it in a bit of white gas, and manually poke through the jet with the stove's cleaning tool, a toothbrush bristle, or a very thin wire. Reassemble the stove, fire it up, and see if the problem is solved. If it's not, move on to check the fuel line.

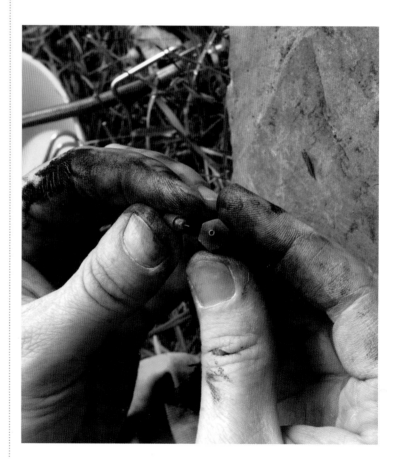

Manually clean the jet by inserting the cleaning needle into the hole. This removes tiny particles, and yes, it is a dirty job!

Clogged fuel line

Inside the fuel line is a long wire cleaning cable. When you remove the fuel line from the bottle, you'll see its tip protruding. Grab onto this tip—with your hand or with pliers if you have them handy—and scour the inside of the fuel line. This simple procedure often loosens the clog and gets you back on track.

If that doesn't work, you're dealing with some serious gunk, and it's time to flush the fuel line. Remove the jet, set it aside, and reassemble the stove (minus the jet). Then pull the cable (some muscle may be required) free of the fuel line and set it aside. Next, attach the fuel bottle to the line and lightly pressurize the bottle (about fifteen strokes). Set the burner over a catch pan and open the control valve, letting about three or four teaspoons of fuel run through the stove. Essentially, this is cleaning out the pipes. Discard the fuel, reinstall the jet and the cable, and fire it up. That elusive blue flame will be yours.

Push the cleaning cable in and out to scour the fuel line clean. Use pliers, your hand, or the cleaning tool that comes with your stove.

With the jet and cleaning cable removed, run a bit of fuel through the system to make it spick-and-span.

This hot, blue flame is what you covet. (Look closely!)

FUEL LEAKING

If fuel leaks from anywhere on the pump or bottle, the likely cause is a damaged O-ring. Disassemble (according to your manual) and lube any dried-out O-rings with either the stuff that came with your stove, cooking oil, or saliva. Reassemble the stove and try again. If the problem persists, it might be that the threads are damaged, and this requires factory intervention.

If the fuel leaks from the jet (located under the burner head), the jet is either not installed properly or damaged. Remove it, inspect it, and be sure to reinstall properly. If the leak continues, it's time to send it in for a full diagnostic.

BOTTLE NOT PRESSURIZING

If no amount of pumping nets pressure inside the bottle (you'll be able to feel it), it's time to dissect the pump assembly and give it a thorough once-over. Follow these steps:

Step 1: Remove the plunger from the pump.

Step 2: Unscrew the fuel tube bushing and inspect the O-ring. Lubricate or replace.

Step 3: Lubricate the rubber pump cup. (On some models the pump cup might be leather.)

Step 4: Check the control valve O-ring. Lubricate or replace.

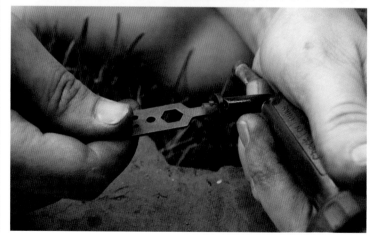

Step 5: The check valve is like a one-way door, letting air flow into the bottle to pressurize it, but preventing fuel from coming through when you pull up on the pump handle. Periodically remove it and wipe it clean.

Tips from the Field: Liquid-Fuel Stoves

With patience, practice, and these key tips, you can master the art of cooking on a liquid-fuel stove.

- **Practice priming:** The vast majority of liquid-fuel stoves need to be primed, or preheated. To do this, release a small puddle of fuel into the priming cup or pad that sits below the generator tube. (Don't overfill it or you'll get a fireball.) Light the fuel, and wait. Once lit, that flame heats the liquid fuel in the generator tube, transforming it to vapor. As the flame begins to burn down, you'll hear a hiss. At this point open the control valve to ignite the stove. Don't rush it and overflood the generator tube, or you'll get a big yellow flame instead of the hot blue one you want.

- **Simmering tricks:** Liquid-fuel stoves are notoriously blowtorch-hot, but simmering is possible. The key: Don't overpressurize the bottle. Before igniting, pump the plunger ten to fifteen times, rather than the standard twenty to thirty. When cooking, be patient with adjustments: Give the stove a minute or so to respond when you turn the adjustment up or down.

- **Estimating fuel needs:** In summer allow three ounces per person per day. In winter bump it up to six ounces. For extremely cold expeditions that require constant snow melting, go with fifteen ounces per person per day.

Canister Stoves

Tiny, light, and beautifully simple, canister stoves are ideal for typical backpackers. They run on pressurized canisters filled with various butane fuel mixes, require no priming (like liquid fuels do), and often ignite without even a match (a push-button starting feature is called a piezo ignition). You can choose a canister stove that has a delicate simmer mode or a volcano that boils water in less than three minutes. Perhaps the best thing about canister stoves: They require practically no maintenance.

PRO FIX

Sometimes stoves can be mysterious. If, despite your best efforts, you can't figure out the problem—or you experience any of these problems—send it back to the manufacturer for a diagnostic.

- Damaged threads at the fuel connection
- Unexplained leaking at the jet
- Damaged fuel line

REAL PEOPLE, REAL PROBLEMS: BENT PIEZO IGNITER

Meg Erznoznik, of Waterford, Michigan, quickly became enamored of her Jetboil Sol-Ti, especially the "fancy little push-button igniter," also known as a piezo. But some careless packing caused Meg's electrode (the metal piece that emits the spark) to get bent out of whack. "When I push the button, I can see the spark, but it doesn't reach the burner anymore. It seems like such a delicate little thing, I was afraid to try to bend it back into shape."

The Fix: Meg is right to be hesitant, but with a little finesse, you can bend that baby back into shape.

Meg Erznoznik chefing up a veggie stir fry in the Michigan woods.

The tiny metal hook (electrode) is bent upward so the spark isn't directed toward the burner.

Use pliers to gently coerce the electrode back into shape.

In its proper form, the spark is pointed down toward the burner. When the control valve is opened, gas is released, and a push of the button brings the stove to life.

Tips from the Field: Canister Stoves

Though supremely simple to use—just turn the knob and light—canister stoves have limitations when it comes to cold weather. Here are some tips to boost their performance in nasty weather:

- Keep the canisters warm at night. Warm fuel vaporizes and burns faster than cold fuel, so tuck canisters in the foot of your sleeping bag while you sleep.
- While cooking in the cold, set the canister in a shallow dish of water.
- If you have a remote canister stove, pressure may decrease as the canister gets low. The flexible fuel line lets you invert the canister to encourage the flow of gas; do this any time you notice a drop in heat output.
- Even if your canister stove has a piezo ignition, don't count on it. They're great when they work, but sometimes they don't (like if the stove gets wet), so always pack a backup source of fire to light your stove.

Canister stoves typically have excellent flame control for recipes that require gentle simmering.

CHAPTER ELEVEN

Hydration

Few things are more important to outdoorspeople than staying hydrated. And, alas, gone are the days when we can cavalierly cup our hands into a running river and slurp away. It might be flowing with microcooties that will set up shop in your intestines and wreak havoc on your digestive system. Why take that risk?

This chapter will solve all your drinking problems: Not only will it teach you how to keep your filter running smoothly (as you'll see from the chart below on water treatment options, filters are really the only ones that require maintenance), you'll also learn how to take care of your water bottles and hydration systems, so they don't turn into smelly, funky breeding grounds.

To render backcountry water safe, you've got several options, each with pros and cons.

TYPE	PROS	CONS
Boiling	Foolproof; kills everything	Time- and fuel-consuming
Chemicals	Ultralight	Needs three to four hours to be effective; some chemicals (iodine) don't kill cryptosporidium; leaves aftertaste
Pump filters	Fast; good for silty water	Heavy; needs regular cleaning and maintenance
Gravity filters	Ideal for large groups, silty water	Slow; for in-camp use only
UV treatment	Fast; light; kills everything	Requires batteries; works only in relatively clear water

Filters

Of all the water treatment methods, filters are certainly the fussiest to deal with, but once you learn the proper techniques, they make a lot of sense.

CLEANING GLASS FIBER

Some filters use pleated glass fiber filter cartridges. The vast surface area inside all those pleats traps both silt (making the water pleasant to drink) and bugs (so you don't get sick). Glass fiber cartridge life varies from brand to brand, but you can extend the life of your cartridge by keeping it clean. When you start to notice that the filter becomes difficult to pump, simply remove the cartridge from the housing and swish it around in a body of water. This loosens the surface debris trapped in the pleats and restores the flow rate.

CLEANING CERAMIC

Some filters use ceramic cartridges. They're heavier, but they last considerably longer than glass fiber ones, and they're also easy to clean. Simply remove the cartridge and give it a good scrub with one of those coarse green kitchen pads (the same ones you use to clean your lasagna pans).

Scrubbing ceramic filters restores the flow rate.

Every so often it's a good idea to fully sterilize your ceramic cartridge, beyond the normal cleaning described above. Read your instruction manual for specific recommendations. Some companies recommend a boiling technique: Remove any O-rings, plop the cartridge into a pot of water, and bring it to a boil. Let it roll for five minutes, then remove the filter and let it dry very thoroughly (three to five days). Other companies recommend pumping a chlorine bleach solution (one capful of bleach per liter of water) through the filter.

BACKFLUSHING

Some filters can be backflushed (check your owner's manual). Essentially, this is running water back through the filter element (opposite from its usual direction) to loosen any sediment. If your filter is backflushable, you'll want to do this anytime the flow rate drops. It's easily done in the field. Just make sure to have your owner's manual with you (or memorized) so you know the drill, which varies from model to model.

LUBRICATING O-RINGS

All filters rely on rubber O-rings to provide tight seals in the piston. Over time O-rings can become gritty, dried out, or cracked. Periodically inspect your O-rings to make sure they're in tip-top shape. Remove them and wipe them free of any dirt. Then rub them with silicone grease or lip balm (saliva even works if you're in a pinch in the field), and reinstall.

FIXING DAMAGED HOSES

Intake and output hoses sometimes sustain injury. If you find a puncture or crack in the hose (you'll know because water will leak out), a few turns of duct tape will solve the problem. If the hose happens to split near the end, simply snip off the damaged part with some scissors and you're back in business.

STORING

Before any long-term storage, take the time to sterilize your filter (all types) by flushing it with a bleach solution. Just mix one capful of bleach with one liter of clean water and pump it through the filter. Then disassemble the filter and let it air-dry thoroughly on a towel for three to five days before storing.

Tips from The Field: Filters

- **Keep it warm:** Extremely cold temps can damage the filter element when residual water freezes inside. When you're expecting cold nights, pack your filter in a zip-top bag (to prevent leaking) and store it in the foot of your sleeping bag.

- **Don't drop it:** A good hard rap on a sharp rock can crack the filter element (especially ceramic), so try to avoid any major fumbles.

- **Start with clean water:** Seek out calm, clear pools rather than roiling streams (where sediment gets stirred up). Don't let the intake hose rest on the bottom of a lake or river. Most filters have an adjustable float on the end of the hose that lets you determine the position of the intake.

- **Let it settle:** If your water source is particularly turbid, you can save your filter some wear and tear by letting it settle. Just scoop up a potful of water and set it aside—even fifteen minutes helps a lot, but wait up to an hour if you're in camp. Then adjust the float so the intake is away from the sediment that has fallen to the bottom, and pump.

- **Don't overuse it:** Remember, all filters have a finite life. There's no need to tax yours by filtering the water that you plan on boiling for your spaghetti dinner.

- **Use a prefilter:** Most filters come with prefilters on the end of the intake hose. If yours doesn't, or if it mysteriously disappeared in the drink, you can build a makeshift one (see photos at right) by wrapping a coffee filter or piece of bandanna around the intake hose and securing with a rubber band.

DUCT TAPE DISPENSER

Wrap your water bottle with a few feet of duct tape, so you'll always have some handy.

The perfect duct tape holder.

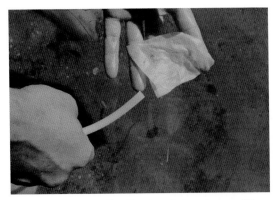

I used a mini paper coffee filter here to jury-rig a pre-filter, but you can cut a section from a standard-size filter or even cut a small piece of fabric from a bandanna or cotton T-shirt.

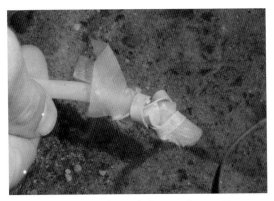

Just cover the end of the intake hose and secure the material with a rubber band. Then pump away.

UV Water Treatment

I've tried most every water-treatment method and device on the market, and for most trips and most conditions, UV treatments (like those made by Steripen) are great. Why? They're super light, they're much faster than chemical treatments (ninety seconds for a liter, compared to thirty minutes to four hours), they don't change the taste of delicious alpine water, and they eliminate all microorganisms (bacteria, protozoa, and viruses), making them a great choice for North American wilderness and developing countries alike.

But there are a few key things to know about keeping a UV pen working properly:

- If your backcountry water is turbid, silty, or otherwise thick with debris, the UV light has trouble penetrating the water. In these cases you have to either prefilter the water (pour it through a bandanna, T-shirt, or coffee filter) or let it settle in a container before pouring off the cleared water and then treating it.

- In cold weather store the device close to your body so the batteries don't get sluggish.

UV light is a fast, easy way to zap your water clean.

- Remember to pack a wide-mouth water bottle because you need to be able to submerge the pen deeply enough so that both sensors are underwater. Otherwise, you'll get a red light/ error message. (**Note:** UV pens only treat small quantities [one to two liters] at a time, so if you need a treatment method for a large group, this may not be it.)

- Handle with care. If you fumble it without the protective lid in place or otherwise pack it carelessly, the glass wand will shatter and you're screwed.
- Pack spare batteries.
- Pack some chemical tablets as a backup.

Hydration Systems

In the world of backpacking, water bottles are like fax machines and hydration systems are like e-mail. Once you start using e-mail, faxing seems inefficient and laborious. It took me a while to jump on the hydration system wagon, but now I'm a firm believer, mainly because with a tube resting handily on my pack's shoulder strap, I drink more regularly, and I can sip in the middle of a huge climb without having to stop and fish out my bottle.

LEAKY BLADDER

Should your bladder bust a seam or get punctured by something sharp, you can seal it back up permanently using Seam Grip. Just make sure the bladder is completely clean and dry, then apply the adhesive (if it's a seam you're fixing, be sure to weight it down with something flat and heavy), and let it cure for twenty-four hours.

CLEANING YOUR SYSTEM

A bleach solution can quickly evict mildew and gunk from bladders, hoses, and bite valves. Fill your system with a half teaspoon of bleach and warm water, then shake. If the smell is particularly bad, let it soak overnight. Then squeeze the bite valve (while holding the bladder high) to flush the hose. If you have a long-handled skinny brush (like a gun-barrel cleaner), give the whole thing a good scrubbing. Then remove the bleach taste with a baking soda rinse (one teaspoon of baking soda per liter of water) and flush once more with water.

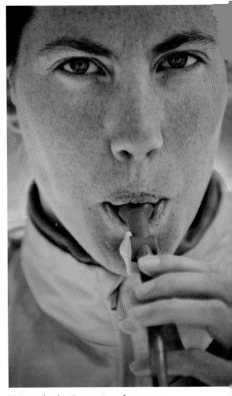

Using a hydration system forces you to drink more, which is always a good thing.

DRYING YOUR SYSTEM

Complete drying of your system's innards is key to preventing that stink from coming back. Convert a plastic coat hanger into the perfect drying rack: Saw off one arm and wrap the rough edges in duct tape. Then stuff a few paper towels inside the reservoir to keep it propped open and hang it to dry.

A homemade contraption like this is great for drying out a hydration bladder. The key is keeping the mouth open so air can circulate.

Tips from the Field: Hydration Systems

- In below-freezing weather, hydration systems tend to freeze up either in the hose or in the bite valve, but there are several preventative tips: Start the day with warm water, buy an insulation kit (it includes a neoprene tube sleeve and bite-valve protector), and remember to push the water back into the reservoir after each sip. You can do this by either blowing into the bite valve until you feel the water exit the hose or holding the bite valve above your head and pinching it open so that gravity forces the water back through the tube.

- When loading your reservoir, place the end with the hose attachment toward the bottom of the pack so gravity lends a hand as you get toward the bottom of your supply.

Note how the hose is looped through a tab on this mom's shoulder strap (upper right). This keeps it from flopping into the dirt when she takes off the pack, which is particularly key when your bite valve doubles as a teething toy.

Hydration systems are great, but we all still need water bottles, for situations like this!

- Make sure to rig an attachment for your bite valve onto your pack's shoulder strap. This way your bite valve doesn't end up in the dirt every time you take off your pack. If your pack doesn't come equipped with a usable loop, rig one using a carabiner, some duct tape, or a loop of cord or webbing.

- Reservoirs close via several different mechanisms: Some are screw-tops, some are zip-tops, and some are fold-over, dry-bag-style tops. No matter what way yours seals, always check it—and then check it again—before loading a full bladder into your pack. Once the system is pressurized between your back and all your other gear, a sloppy seal could spell a disastrous leak—all over your sleeping bag.

De-Funking Your Water Bottles

Especially if you use your bottles for energy drinks, whiskey, or wine, they can get stinky and stained. Here are a few tips to restore them to their former glory.

- Remove musty smells and tastes with this solution: the juice of one lemon, a few tablespoons of white vinegar, and a few tablespoons of baking soda. Let the solution soak overnight, then run your bottle through the dishwasher.

- For really pesky smells try wrapping a charcoal briquette in newspaper. Insert it into your bottle, screw on the cap, and let it sit for a few days. The charcoal should absorb any remaining odor.

- Most bottles are dishwasher safe. Just be sure to place them far away from the heating element, which can melt the plastic parts.

- To remove wine stains, fill the bottle with a cup of liquid bleach and water, and let it sit overnight.

- Always store bottles (and bladders) with tops off to promote airflow.

- For extra mildew protection, store your bottles or bladders in the freezer, where nothing can grow.

Kids of all ages—including my son Joey, pictured here—love hydration systems, and moms do too, because it encourages frequent slurping to keep them well hydrated.

CHAPTER TWELVE

Trekking Poles

More and more hikers are toting trekking poles, and with good reason: They absorb shock with each step, improve your balance, and help you safely cross streams and snowfields. Plus, they come in handy around camp for tarp pitching and bear-bag hanging. A good pair of trekking poles is a fairly big investment these days, but the good news is that they're almost entirely fixable, with affordable replacement parts. This chapter will explain all the fix-it techniques for the two main types of today's collapsible trekking poles: twist-lock and snap-lock.

Collapsing Sections

Have you ever planted your pole only to stumble or fall when it collapses? Man, I hate when that happens! The cause? The sections slip due to wear, tear, dirt, and grit inside the pole sections, all of which can be minimized and solved with some easy tricks.

TWIST-LOCK POLES

Understanding how this type of pole works will help you avoid problems, which often result from frantic twisting that gets you nowhere. Inside the end of each section is a screw that feeds into an expander plug. Twist the shaft, and it forces that expander open so that it locks firmly against the inside of the pole shaft. Frantic twisting can cause overloosening, and it might seem like the pole is shot. Chances are it's not: Just pull the bottom pole section out so that just the end of the expander is revealed, and carefully rescrew it back in place.

With this type of pole, problems generally arise from one of two things: Either the inside of the shaft is dirty (see "Care and Maintenance") or the expander is lacking in friction or otherwise worn down.

This expander plug widens as you twist the pole sections, creating a friction lock against the inside of the other pole section.

Try lightly sanding a slipping expander plug to boost friction.

Pull the pole section apart and inspect the expander. If you can see that it's worn down around the edges, a replacement will do the trick. Order a pair from the manufacturer (a lot less money than new poles) and snap it into place. Or try creating a little extra friction: Lightly sand the circumference of the expander, creating horizontal striations. Wipe it clean and reinstall to see if that did the trick.

SNAP-LOCK POLES

I'm a big fan of this type of pole because the mechanism is on the outside, so there's nothing mysterious. Snap-lock poles feature a plastic clamp that tensions around the pole section with a simple screw adjustment. Over time that screw can loosen, so just be sure to have a multitool in your pocket. A quick half turn usually does the trick!

Keep this screw snug, but not overly tight, or the clamp won't snap.

REAL PEOPLE, REAL PROBLEMS:
BENT TREKKING POLES

Mike Browning, of Franklin Park, New Jersey, was in the middle of a 20-mile weekend loop hike in the Catskills when the tip of one of his two-year-old REI Shocklite poles became lodged between two boulders. "I couldn't get my hands free in time, so I fell over and my pole paid the price. The bottom section was good and bent and the pole would no longer collapse completely."

Mike Browning crosses Sugarloaf Creek in Kings Canyon National Park in California.

The Fix: Lucky for Mike, his pole was bent in a nice, clean arc, so the prognosis was good. (If it bends abruptly or if the aluminum kinks even a tiny bit, that pole section is toast.) The key is to gently, ever-so-gently, try to reshape the pole. I tried a bunch of different techniques. What worked best was a combination of lightly tapping the bend with a large rock and prying it back between two rocks. I succeeded in getting the pole almost completely straight again—certainly straight enough to hike with. The bottom section is about 4 inches shy of being able to collapse completely, but it's totally serviceable and I didn't want to risk breaking it by working on it anymore.

First, try using a big rock to gently tap-tap-tap the bulging section.

Next, try jamming the end of the bent section between two rocks or in the crook of a tree and gently pull back to straighten.

Replacement Parts

POLE SECTIONS

If you bend a section beyond repair (if it's kinked or if your attempts at rebending it don't work), don't ditch the whole pole: Order a replacement section from the manufacturer. It will take all of two minutes to replace and won't cost a lot.

TIPS

Hiking pole tips are generally made of carbide, a super-tough compound of carbon and heavy metals designed to stand up to constant scraping on rocks. Eventually, though, carbide wears down. Pole tips have a convex shape—the edges around the circle help provide grip to keep the poles from skidding out from under you. When the edges wear down and the tip becomes concave, it's time for replacement (around $20 per pair).

Some tips are a simple pressure fit: Just pull it off with pliers and insert the new one. Others use adhesive and require you to heat up the joint (in boiling water) so you can pull it free. Then just apply hot-melt craft glue to the new tip and reinstall.

BASKETS

The nice thing about splurging for a good pair of collapsible poles is that you can use them all year round—for skiing and snowshoeing as well as hiking. Many poles come with a couple sets of baskets, but sometimes you have to buy them separately. They generally come in three varieties (see photo).

Care and Maintenance

Especially with twist-lock poles, where the mechanism is hidden inside the shaft, it's really, really important to keep them dry, clean, and free of gunk. Don't be afraid to pull your poles apart and clean them, especially after trips. Never use soap or water to clean your poles, and never use any sort of lubricant. Instead, try the methods shown in the top two photos at right.

Customize your pole basket to the task at hand. Clockwise from top: a standard snow basket, a trekking basket, and a deep-powder basket.

Use a dry toothbrush to clean the threads and the expander plug.

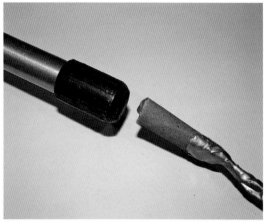

Clean the interior of the female pole ends with a coarse gun-barrel brush, a toothbrush, or a dry rag attached to a coat-hanger wire. Tape a plug of sandpaper to a dowel or coat hanger, and twist it horizontally to create striations that will improve friction.

Also, if you use your poles in hot weather, periodically wash the grips and straps with soap and water, so they don't attract critters like an all-you-can-eat buffet.

This little pika found itself a tasty snack in this strap's sweat deposits. Keep your straps salt-free by scrubbing them down with soap and water once a year or so.

Push-Button Staffs

Single hiking staffs often have a simple push-button mechanism. Keep them in good working order using the same methods you would use for twist-lock poles. One notable difference: Because there are no expander plugs inside, you can use a lubricant (like WD-40) if the buttons get sticky. Also, check the shaft regularly for cracks that can appear around the adjustment holes. If you find one, contact the manufacturer for a replacement section immediately.

Many single hiking staffs adjust via a simple push-button system.

Make a Low-Impact Pole Tip

Most times you want that reassuring bite that a carbide tip provides. But sometimes, like on my recent hike in Utah's Capitol Reef National Park, pole tips can scar the gorgeous red rock, and it can tear up the delicate cryptobiotic soil. In situations like these it's good hiking etiquette to put rubber feet on your poles. Some companies sell these accessories, but you can easily make your own, using duct tape and a pair of rubber cane tips (at any drug store).

Step 1: Put the cane tip over the pole tip to judge how far up you need to wrap the duct tape. Mark it.

Step 2: Split the tape and wrap it around the pole until you can get a solid pressure fit with the cane tip.

Step 3: Shove the cane tip firmly over the duct tape, as far up as it will go.

Step 4: Secure the tip with another wrap of tape, and twist it against the pole tip for maximum adhesion.

Step 5: Add a final wrap of tape around the pole tip.

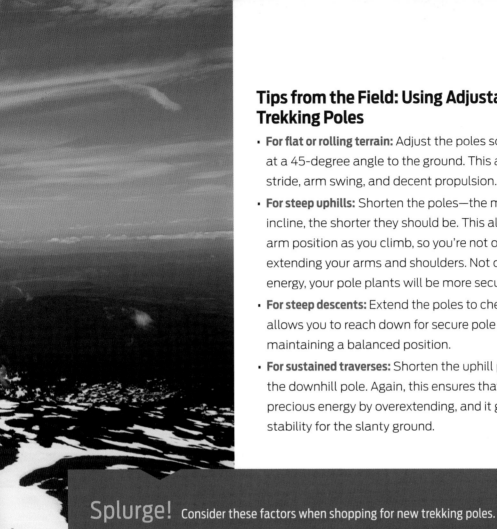

Tips from the Field: Using Adjustable Trekking Poles

- **For flat or rolling terrain:** Adjust the poles so that your elbow is at a 45-degree angle to the ground. This allows for a natural stride, arm swing, and decent propulsion.

- **For steep uphills:** Shorten the poles—the more dramatic the incline, the shorter they should be. This allows for a natural arm position as you climb, so you're not overreaching or over-extending your arms and shoulders. Not only will you save energy, your pole plants will be more secure.

- **For steep descents:** Extend the poles to chest height, which allows you to reach down for secure pole placements while maintaining a balanced position.

- **For sustained traverses:** Shorten the uphill pole and lengthen the downhill pole. Again, this ensures that you're not wasting precious energy by overextending, and it gives you the most stability for the slanty ground.

Splurge! Consider these factors when shopping for new trekking poles.

PICK THIS . . .	OR THAT
Aluminum: Durable and affordable	**Carbon fiber:** Ultralight but pricier
Plastic grips: Rugged and inexpensive but get slippery with sweat	**Rubber or cork grips:** More comfortable and secure but more expensive
Two sections: Less expensive and have one less potential failure point	**Three sections:** Pack down much smaller but usually cost more
Shock absorbers: Reduce impact and add comfort but increase price	**Nonshock:** Less expensive and slightly lighter

Adjust your hiking pole length on the fly to suit the terrain.

CHAPTER THIRTEEN

Lights

Lights are a pretty low-maintenance category. Buy a good one and it will last you a lifetime, especially with today's LED (light-emitting diode) bulbs, which typically last for 100,000 hours (or eleven years). LEDs also consume less power, which means that you'll be burning far fewer batteries, and saving money.

Care and Maintenance

Follow these tips to keep your light shining bright:

- Store your light with the batteries removed. This does several things: It prolongs the life of your batteries and eliminates the chance of corrosion buildup during long-term storage.

- Remove dead batteries immediately. Dead batteries are much more likely to leak (and corrode) than fresh ones.

- Apply a thin film of dielectric silicone grease to the contacts to prevent corrosion. You can find small packets of it on the cheap at auto parts stores.

- Choose the right batteries. We have so many choices these days—lithium-ion, NiMH, alkaline. It's key to read your owner's manual and know what kind of battery the manufacturer recommends. Using the wrong type can damage the lamp's circuitry.

- Install the batteries correctly, making note of the + and − marks on the battery ends and the casing. It sounds super simple, but most modern LEDs will actually work for a little while with the polarities reversed. Over time, though, the light will overheat and the circuitry will become damaged.

- Don't mix fresh with old batteries or rechargeables with alkalines. Performance can suffer in the short term, and wreak big-time havoc on the circuitry in the long term.

Spent batteries should be disposed of properly so they don't leak toxic stuff into the ground at the landfill. Check with your local public works department for the scoop in your town.

- Periodically check that the contacts are not bent or tweaked. (This can happen when a battery is inserted backwards or if a light is dropped.) If they are, gently push them back to shape.

The end of a flat screwdriver works perfectly for straightening battery contacts.

- When it's cold out, snuggle with your light. Batteries work much better when they're warm, so store them in your bag at night or in a pocket next to your body.

Corrosion

If your headlamp or flashlight gets wet and water finds its way into the battery pack, the contacts can develop corrosion, which often manifests itself in a vivid blue gunk where the battery meets the metal contacts. You can prevent this by immediately drying out your lamp after its dowsing: Just open the battery pack, remove the batteries, and towel-dry the inner chamber as well as the batteries. Let it rest for a few hours with the pack open so any residual moisture can evaporate.

REMOVING CORROSION

Corrosion prevents the battery from connecting properly to the contacts, but all you need to do is get rid of it. Don't introduce any (more) liquid to the light, but use a dry, stiff metal brush or some sandpaper to gently scrub it off.

See that pretty blue stuff on the right-side battery contacts? That's corrosion, stemming from dampness inside the battery pack.

Remove all visible corrosion and be sure that you didn't bend the contacts in the process.

Splurge!

Headlamps are really the way to go for hikers and campers. Why hold a flashlight when you can strap one to your head and have it follow your every gaze? If you're in the market for a new illuminator, consider these factors:

Light output: Measured in lumens, this is the total amount of light the lamp emits (1 lumen equals the light of 1 candle from 1 foot away). For basic camping and on-trail hiking, a device with 24 lumens is plenty. On trickier terrain—scrambles, off-trail routes, and canyons—invest in a lamp with 55 lumens or more. Cyclists and cavers might require 100-plus-lumen lamps—some floodlight models even deliver a whopping 350. But beware: Lumens reveal nothing about the beam's quality, or how well it illuminates a distant object. If the lamp has poor optics, for example, it might diffuse the light in many directions, rather than in a useful, focused beam, so consider beam distance as well.

Beam distance: This is the max distance the lamp usefully illuminates something (see above). Your lamp should shine 25 meters for basic trail hiking and 45-plus meters for climbing, orienteering, running, etc.

Light source: Unless you're a caver, opt for LEDs over halogen bulbs. They're not as bright, but they last much longer and won't break.

Batteries: Some tiny lamps use coin-cell or camera batteries; these cut weight but not enough to justify hunting for these rarer battery types. For most uses, stick with regular alkaline or rechargeables. In cold weather use lithium-ion batteries, which work well down to −20 degrees F or more. Alkaline batteries get sluggish in the cold, and lose power 60 percent faster at 0 degrees F than at 68 degrees F.

Power usage: Decide if you want a lamp with regulated or unregulated power. The former keeps the light output constant until the battery can't support it; then output plummets to emergency light (some have low-battery indicators). Unregulated lamps slowly dim as the batteries lose juice, lowering beam distance but warning you of waning power.

Modes: Here's a rundown of useful settings to look for:

- High/low power: All but the most basic lamps let you choose between brightest (sucks the most juice) and economy mode (dimmer, but saves power). Some also offer a medium setting.

- Focused or wide-angle beam: Typically, narrow beams travel farther than wide-angle ones, which disperse light into a broader area. Some headlamps convert between the two, either by using a diffuser lens to change the beam angle or by activating peripheral LEDs.

- Extra-strength pulses: Some models let you amp light output by 50 percent for up to twenty seconds, gulping power but giving you a glimpse far ahead.

- Strobe: Flashing lights signal rescuers.

- Color LEDs: These (red or green) lights preserve night vision—the eyes' adjustment to low light. Full adaptation takes thirty minutes, and bright light destroys it. Avoid lamps with a tinted screen you pull over white LEDs; this only dulls the light.

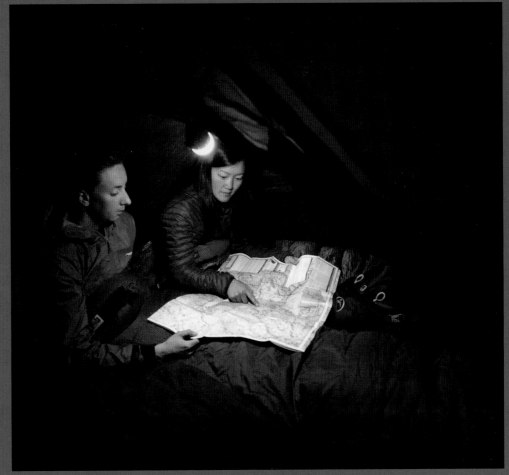

Some headlamps can transform into a lantern for a more ambient light.

CHAPTER FOURTEEN

Odds and Ends

Cameras

Cameras—especially DSLRs (Digital Single Lens Reflex cameras)—are one of the most sensitive items a hiker is likely to carry, not to mention a huge investment. This section will teach you how to handle your camera in the field (even in really nasty weather) and how to give it a good cleaning once you get back home.

TIPS FROM THE FIELD: CAMERAS

1. Carry your camera in a padded case to guard against scratches, dirt, and sweat.

2. If your camera takes lens filters, use a neutral skylight/ UV filter to prevent lens scratches.

3. If you need to change a lens in the field, do it quickly, and face away from wind or rain to keep the camera's innards clean and protected.

4. When hiking in deluge conditions or serious sandstorms, use a raincover on your case, or store the camera inside your pack.

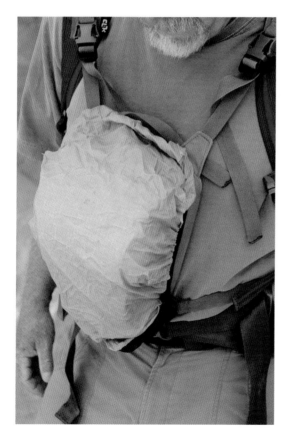

5. If your case does get wet, sun-dry the interior as soon as possible to prevent humidity from being forced into the camera by external heat.

6. Dirty cases just force grit and oils into your camera. Machine-wash them regularly on gentle cycle, no soap, with zips open. Let them air-dry overnight or longer.

7. During trail rests put the camera case on top of your backpack to keep dirt off the case.

8. Around camp hang your camera case off a tripod or tree branch.

9. For dramatic photos in wind or sandstorms, make an impromptu cover with zip-top bags and tape. Vent it regularly, or tuck a few desiccant packets inside to prevent condensation.

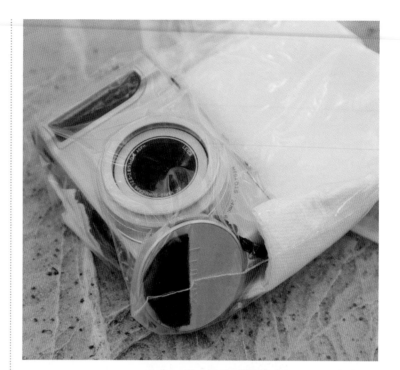

10. If your camera gets seriously wet, you can try to save it by quickly putting it in a zip-top bag with desiccant packets and/or dry paper towels or toilet tissue. Then suck all the air out and seal it. Moisture will (hopefully) be drawn out of the camera.

11. If lenses get interior condensation, take the lens cap off and set them facing straight at the sun. In most conditions the internal fog will clear in minutes.

CLEANING YOUR CAMERA

All cameras—DSLRs or point-and-shoots—need maintenance. Here's how the pros methodically clean their cameras, so they're always ready for the next big sunset.

Step 1: Wipe off the camera's exterior using a damp, lint-free cloth like a clean, well-used cotton T-shirt or bandanna.

Step 2: Remove LCD screen and eyepiece covers and clean beneath them.

Step 3: Use a damp cotton swab to remove grit from complex seams and cracks.

Step 4: Extend zoom lenses to expose internal barrel parts and clean beneath them.

Step 5: Clean grit and grease off lens and camera body mounts, and the electrical contacts on them, using a damp cloth.

Step 6: To clean lenses, first blow off as much grit as possible using a squeeze bulb or canned air. Don't neglect the rear elements, which are more important to image quality than the lens front. Then use a lens brush or soft camel-hair art paintbrush to remove more stubborn particles.

Step 7: Wipe a moistened microfiber cloth (unlike cotton, microfiber won't scratch the lens) gently around the lens elements. Examine lens elements in full sunlight and repeat until they're smudge-free.

Step 8: Lens caps get very dirty over time, contaminating the lenses they were designed to protect. Clean them using water and cotton swabs.

GEARHEAD PROJECT: MAKE A SURVIVAL BRACELET

Not only do these bracelets look cool and make great gifts for your favorite hiker, they're pretty smart, too, and a great wrist adornment for any DIY gearhead (which I assume you are, or you wouldn't be reading this book). In an emergency you can use the paracord for lashings, tourniquets, shoelaces, snares, tying splints, or, if you tease out the fibers, even fishing line or sewing thread. To make a bracelet, you'll need scissors, a lighter, a tape measure, and 10 feet of 550-weight paracord (choose a color you like).

Step 1: Cut a 2-foot length of cord, melt the ends, and fold it in half. Wrap the doubled-up cord around your wrist. Pull the tag ends through the loop. Tie an overhand knot with the ends. Adjust the knot so you can slip a finger between the cord and your wrist.

Step 2: Lay the remaining 8 feet of cord in front of you horizontally. Now place the base cord, with the loop at the top, over the middle of the 8-foot cord, forming a T.

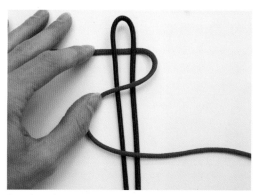

Step 3: Make a cobra knot. To start, take the cord on the right and bring it over the top of the base cord to form a Z.

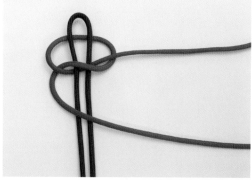

Step 4: Take the left cord and thread it down through the loop on the left side of the base cord. Go under the base cord and up inside the loop on the right. Pull tight.

Step 5: Make sure the overhand knot will fit through the small loop at the top of the base cord. Next, starting on the left, reverse the process. Begin by, this time, making an S.

Step 6: To finish reversing the step, bring the right cord down through the loop to the right of the base cord. Go under the base cord and up inside the loop on the left. Pull tight.

Step 7: You've now completed the first cobra knot. Continue making cobra knots until you are about ¼ inch from the stopper knot.

Step 8: Check the fit on your wrist by pushing the stopper knot through the loop at the apex. You can adjust the fit by moving the knot up or down. The bracelet should fit snugly without being too tight. When you're done, trim all four tag ends and melt them.

Step 9: To wear, push the stopper knot through the loop to hold the bracelet securely on your wrist. If desired, you can substitute wooden toggles, buttons, buckles, and other fastening methods for the knot. To use the cord, simply unweave the bracelet.

Gaiters

These boot-and-ankle protectors really take a beating, especially when used with skis or crampons. But I've had the same pair of gaiters for about fifteen years, and they're still going strong because I've taken good care of them. Here's how:

- Periodically inspect your underfoot straps. Are they fraying? Snip off any loose threads. Are they wearing through or in danger of becoming detached? Most gaiter straps are replaceable. If they attach via buckles, just contact the manufacturer for some replacements that you can install. If they're sewn on and you're not confident in your sewing skills (like me), send them back to the manufacturer for a bomber repair job.

- Clean the Velcro. Most gaiters rely on a large swath of Velcro either up the front or down the side of the gaiter. These closures allow for easy on and off, but if the seal isn't solid, then water can penetrate. If your Velcro gets gunked up (and it will), give it a good cleaning using the technique described in Chapter 2.

- Once a season give them a bath and a good spray with a waterproofing treatment. Chapter 2 has all the details.

My favorite gaiters (Outdoor Research Crocs): Fifteen years and still going strong, thanks to bomber fabrics, tough urethane-coated (and replaceable) nylon underfoot straps, and extra-wide swaths of Velcro that form a super-tight seal against the elements.

Crampons

SHARPENING

Mountaineers rely on the toothy bite of their crampons on ice and snow. But over time, because they're often used over mixed terrain (snow, ice, and rocks), the teeth wear down and become dull. A periodic sharpening keeps them in good fighting form. You'll need a standard hand file (do not use any type of grinding wheel, as tempting as it is, because it generates too much heat and can change the temper of the metal) and either a vise grip to hold the crampon still or a leather work glove to protect your holding hand.

Use a long, downward stroke to file both sides of the teeth. Don't file the broad sides of the teeth, but rather the thin sides that lead to the point. You don't need to take it down to a super-fine point, which will just wear down quicker, but the teeth should be pointed enough to penetrate ice.

STORING

After a season of use, give your dry crampons a light spray with WD-40 to prevent rust. Store them in a padded case to protect your newly sharpened points.

Climbing Ropes

Not only is a rope a pretty sizable investment, it's also a critical piece of safety gear that needs some special TLC.

CLEANING

If your rope starts to look grimy or feels gritty, it's time for a wash. Believe it or not, little dirt particles left on a rope sheath can work their way inside and cause abrasion and premature wear. Fill a big wash basin with cold water and a couple ounces of ReviveX Climbing Rope Cleaner Concentrate (or a mild liquid dish soap). Swish and agitate the rope for about five minutes, then let it sit for another five. Remove the rope and give it a rinse with the garden hose. Let it air-dry uncoiled in a shady place.

TIPS FROM THE FIELD: ROPES

When you're out in the backcountry, keep these rope-care tips in mind:

- **Tread carefully:** Avoid stepping on your rope; this works dirt into the fibers and causes undue wear.
- **Keep it dry:** Ropes lose up to 30 percent of their strength when they're wet (they regain their strength when dry).
- **Coil it:** Learn the proper coiling method, so you can carry and store your rope kink-free.
- **Avoid the sun:** Climbing with your rope on sunny days will do no harm, but don't use it to rig a line or a long-term belay or toprope and let it bake for days on end. This degrades the materials and weakens the rope.
- **Replace them:** Ropes don't last forever. They should be replaced after any big fall or every four to five years with occasional use.

When your rope team gathers up at rest stops, pull your partners in and coil the rope to avoid trips and hang-ups.

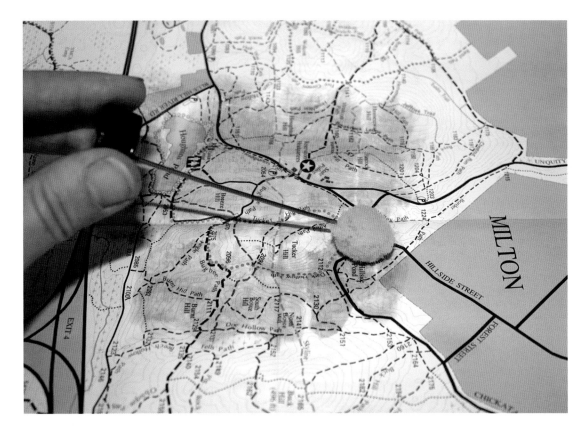

Maps

WATERPROOFING

Want to get more miles out of your maps? Whenever possible, keep them stored in a zip-top bag when you're on the trail. Or waterproof them using Aquaseal Map Seal. Use the included applicator to paint a thin coating of the sealant over one side of the map. Once it gets tacky (in about five minutes), repeat the procedure. When that side is totally dry, flip the map over and repeat on side two. Hang the map from a line, using clothespins or binder clips, and let it cure for seventy-two hours. Then you can fold your map, draw on it with a pencil, refold it, and otherwise use it, without worrying about a few drops of rain.

One four-ounce bottle of Aquaseal Map Seal will treat three or four topo maps, depending on their size.

Sunglasses

SCRATCHES

I've tried about a dozen different homespun remedies to remove scratches from sunglass lenses (both glass and polycarbonate)—everything from toothpaste to Brasso to a paste made from ground mustard and vinegar. Bottom line: Nothing works. Once a scratch, always a scratch. The best we can do is not give scratches a chance to happen!

CLEANING AND STORING

We've all done it: grabbed the edge of our cotton T-shirt and scrubbed the lenses of our shades with thumb and forefinger. But that's how you get those little micro-scratches that eventually cloud your expensive lenses. Instead, follow these sunglass care tips (these tips also apply to binoculars, monoculars, or any other optical equipment):

- Do not use any wood-based product (tissue or paper towels) for cleaning. Instead, use a soft, clean chamois or microfiber cloth. Most every new pair of sunglasses comes with one, so use it!

- Always moisten the lenses before cleaning. Lens-cleaning solution is great, but even a few drops of water will do. This prevents any particles from scratching the lens.

- Especially when backpacking, bring a hard-sided case for your shades. On those cloudy days when you don't need them on your face, they'll stay safe and sound inside their protective cocoon, which can get tossed into your pack without much thought.

THE 10 ESSENTIALS

Hikers love to debate this classic list, which was designed back in the 1930s by The Mountaineers, a Seattle-based climbing club that to this day leads members on adventures. The purpose of the list was, and still is, to ensure that hikers could react and respond to an accident or emergency and remain safe if forced to spend an unplanned night or two in the wilds. Here's the list, which should always be part of your arsenal, whether it's for a day hike or a big, weeklong adventure.

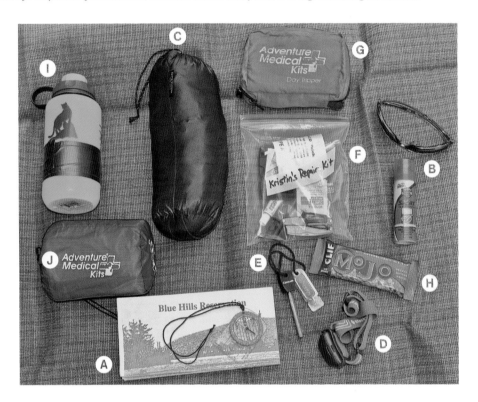

A. **Navigation:** map and compass or GPS

B. **Sun protection:** sunglasses and sunscreen

C. **Insulation:** a warm jacket

D. **Illumination:** headlamp or flashlight

E. **Fire:** waterproof matches, lighter, or magnesium fire starter

F. **Repair kit:** see Chapter 1

G. **First-aid supplies**

H. **Nutrition:** extra food

I. **Hydration:** extra water or the means to treat backcountry water (see Chapter 11)

J. **Emergency shelter:** bivy sack, tarp, or emergency blanket

LEAVE NO TRACE PRINCIPLES

Everyone knows not to litter in the wilderness, but some boneheads do it anyways. Leave No Trace is a nonprofit group devoted to teaching people how to enjoy the outdoors responsibly—and it goes way beyond littering. Their philosophy entails seven principles, which we should all engrave into our personal backcountry ethic.

1. Plan Ahead and Prepare

- Know the regulations and special concerns for the area you plan to visit.
- Prepare for extreme weather, hazards, and emergencies.
- Schedule your trip to avoid times of high use.
- Visit in small groups. Split larger parties into groups of four to six.
- Repackage food to minimize waste.
- Use a map and compass to eliminate the use of marking paint, rock cairns, or flagging.

2. Travel and Camp on Durable Surfaces

- Durable surfaces include established trails and campsites, rock, gravel, dry grasses, or snow.
- Protect riparian areas by camping at least 200 feet from lakes and streams.
- Good campsites are found, not made. Altering a site is not necessary. In popular areas:
    - Concentrate use on existing trails and campsites.
    - Keep campsites small.
    - Focus activity in areas where vegetation is absent.
- In pristine areas:
    - Disperse use to prevent the creation of campsites and trails.
    - Walk single file in the middle of the trail, even when wet or muddy.
    - Avoid places where impacts are just beginning.

3. Dispose of Waste Properly

- Pack it in, pack it out. Inspect your campsite and rest areas for trash or spilled foods. Pack out all trash, leftover food, and litter.
- Deposit solid human waste in cat holes dug 6 to 8 inches deep at least 200 feet from water, campsites, and trails. Cover and disguise the cat hole when finished.

- Pack out toilet paper and hygiene products.
- To wash yourself or your dishes, carry water 200 feet away from streams or lakes and use small amounts of biodegradable soap. Scatter strained dishwater.

4. Leave What You Find

- Preserve the past: Examine, but do not touch, cultural or historic structures and artifacts.
- Leave rocks, plants, and other natural objects as you find them.
- Avoid introducing or transporting nonnative species.
- Do not build structures or furniture or dig trenches.

5. Minimize Campfire Impacts

- Campfires can cause lasting impacts to the backcountry. Use a lightweight stove for cooking and enjoy a candle lantern for light.
- Where fires are permitted, use established fire rings, fire pans, or mound fires.
- Keep fires small. Only use sticks from the ground that can be broken by hand.
- Burn all wood and coals to ash, put out campfires completely, then scatter cool ashes.

6. Respect Wildlife

- Observe wildlife from a distance. Do not follow or approach them.
- Never feed animals. Feeding wildlife damages their health, alters natural behaviors, and exposes them to predators and other dangers.
- Protect wildlife and your food by storing rations and trash securely.
- Control pets at all times, or leave them at home.
- Avoid wildlife during sensitive times: mating, nesting, raising young, and during the winter.

7. Be Considerate of Other Visitors

- Respect other visitors and protect the quality of their experience.
- Be courteous. Yield to other users on the trail.
- Step to the downhill side of the trail when encountering pack stock.
- Take breaks and camp away from trails and other visitors.
- Let nature's sounds prevail. Avoid loud voices and noises.

For more information on this great organization, visit its website www.LNT.org.

CHAPTER FIFTEEN

Duct Tape Ingenuity

Entire books have been written about the virtues of duct tape and all the glorious things it can do. To be sure, duct tape is a must on any backcountry trip. This short chapter pays homage to the ubiquitous silver tape, and to some clever people who have used it wisely.

Duct Tape Magic

Sure, it can help you fix a broken tent pole or tape up a hole in your little ditty bag. But here are some other clever ways to use it:

Problem: Sore hips from an inadequately padded hipbelt
Solution: Tape a T-shirt, a folded bandanna, or some other piece of soft fabric to each hipbelt pad.

Problem: Broken sunglasses
Solution: Tape them up!

Problem: Close encounter with a cactus
Solution: Gently press a piece of tape over the area and pull away all the spines at once.

Problem: Boot laces that won't stay tied
Solution: Lace them up tight, then tape them down.

Problem: Broken zipper pull
Solution: Feed a thin strip of duct tape through the hole on the slider, then wrap it with a few large pieces to create a big, glove-friendly zipper pull (see photo at right).

Problem: Broken plastic buckle
Solution: If you don't have a spare in your repair kit, wrap the buckle securely with duct tape for a temporary fix.

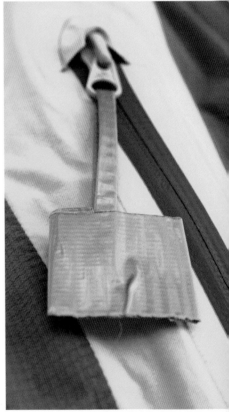

When fashioning a zipper pull, bigger is better, so you can easily grab it with gloves on.

REAL PEOPLE, REAL PROBLEMS: FORGOTTEN HAT

Paige Boucher, of Steamboat Springs, Colorado, was enjoying a sunny weekend ski-touring hut-to-hut near Breckenridge, Colorado, when she realized that she forgot to pack her visor. "I'm a hat person and rarely leave home without a sun hat, but somehow I spaced out on this trip," she says. "Fortunately, I did not forget the beer. After pondering the situation and realizing that I had the tools I needed to fashion my own visor, I was back in business after fifteen minutes. And no sunburned face!"

Paige Boucher models her Moosehead beer can hat.

1. Carefully cut a visor shape out of an empty can with your pocketknife scissors.

2. Tape the sharp edge with a length of duct tape.

3. Enlist a friend to help you fit another length of duct tape (folded over so it sticks to itself, not your hair) to your head size. Voila!

Problem: Split or punctured water filter or hydration system hose
Solution: Apply a few turns of duct tape.

Problem: Bugs eating you alive
Solution: Seal up your shirt and pants by wrapping the cuffs with duct tape at your wrists and ankles.

Problem: Forgot your water bottle
Solution: Buy a bottle of water at a trailhead convenience store and reinforce it by wrapping the whole thing with duct tape. The tape will strengthen it and prevent dents, cracks, and leaks.

Problem: Wet clothes
Solution: Make a duct tape clothesline by twisting a long swath into a rope. String between two trees and hang your stuff.

Problem: Forgot your camp shoes
Solution: Cover your socks with duct tape and pad around camp without getting wet.

Problem: Hands-free lighting without a headlamp
Solution: Wrap a few turns of duct tape around the end of your mini flashlight. Now you can hold it firmly between your teeth.

REAL PEOPLE, REAL PROBLEMS: FORGOTTEN SPOON

Mike Nancarrow, from Jacksonville, Florida, was hiking high on Blood Mountain in Georgia. When he stopped for his mac 'n' cheese lunch, he realized that he was spoonless. "I found a forked stick, wrapped it with some tape from my hiking pole stash, and shot this photo for posterity!" Starvation averted!

As effective as the finest sterling silver.

My buddy **Steve Howe,** from Torrey, Utah, has hiked thousands of miles—carrying packs that would make normal men weep—through some of the craziest, remotest backcountry in the world. He has super-wide feet, which has always made boot fitting a challenge. Because of this, he's had way more than his fair share of blisters. Bad ones, too. But he's never let that stop him. Instead, he came up with this elaborate, but hugely successful, blister remedy using duct tape. "I've doctored up my own feet dozens of times, and I've earned the undying love and gratitude of loads of other hikers by teaching them how," Steve says. "This little trick can literally be a trip saver."

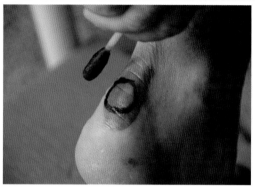

Step 1: Clean the area and apply tincture of benzoin around the blister to help everything stick better. (**Note:** Black circle added for reference.)

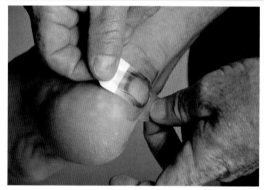

Step 2: For open blisters apply Glacier Gel (a blister pad from Adventure Medical Kits) stretched over the blister with as few wrinkles as possible.

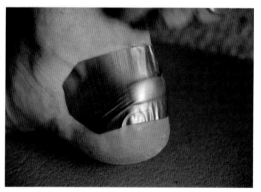

Step 3: Keep your ankle flexed forward during this taping procedure. Start by tightly stretching a 6- to 8-inch piece of duct tape horizontally over the blister. Round the edges to keep it from peeling.

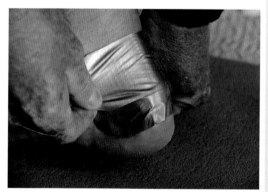

Step 4: Stretch several more pieces in the same direction.

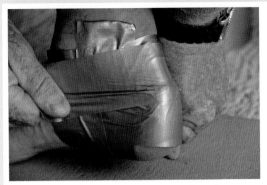

Step 5: Layer tape in both directions until you have a smooth, tight wrap that covers the heel pocket completely. Wrap well forward of your ankle bone, but not far above it.

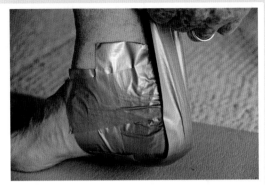

Step 6: Finish the wraps with one or two sections of tape running down the Achilles and underfoot. This keeps heel lift friction from rolling and peeling the horizontal tape bands.

Step 7: Hold the assembly in place by running one or two half widths of duct tape around your heel and across the forward fold of your ankle.Tilt your shin forward during this, to prevent uncomfortable tension while walking.

Step 8: To finish, trim up any uneven edges and awkward folds with scissors. While hiking, you may need to trim back tape from the Achilles, shin, and forefoot to avoid irritation. Avoid wet-footed river fords, since they'll loosen the whole blister repair.

Step 9: On multiday trips remove the tape overnight to let your foot breathe. To save time and make tape last longer, cut the instep strap and carefully remove the tape bootie for reuse. A short piece of tape will reattach it.

EDITORS' CHOICE AWARDS
BACKPACKER
THE OUTDOORS AT YOUR DOORSTEP®

Gear Guide

425 TRAIL-TESTED PRODUCTS & CAMPING TIPS

26 SWEET DEALS!
TESTER PICKS IN EVERY CATEGORY

YOUR LIGHTEST LOAD EVER!
WHAT TO BUY, HOW TO PACK

SHOP SMART
EXPERT ADVICE ON FIT, FEATURES, AND FABRICS

MAKE YOUR GEAR LAST FOREVER
66 CHEAP, EASY FIXES

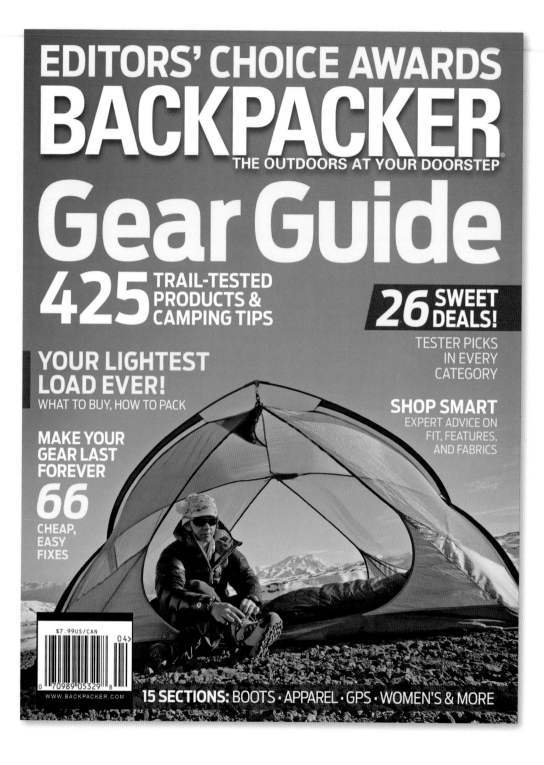

15 SECTIONS: BOOTS · APPAREL · GPS · WOMEN'S & MORE

Resources

BACKPACKER MAGAZINE

Tons of fresh content—videos, photos, articles—on gear repair, maintenance, and selection, as well as everything else you need to know about the outdoors.

www.backpacker.com

SUPPLIES

Aquaseal

Maker of all manner of waterproofing products

17631 147th St. SE, #7

Monroe, WA 98272

(360) 794-8250

www.aquaseal.com

Grangers

UK-based company that makes cleaning and waterproofing products

Grange Close

Clover Nook Industrial Park

Alfreton, Derbyshire, UK DE55 4QT

44 (0) 1773 521 521

www.grangers.co.uk

McNett Corporation

Maker of Seam Grip and loads of other great care and repair products

1411 Meador Ave.

Bellingham, WA 98229

(360) 671-2227

www.mcnett.com

Nikwax

Maker of waterproofing and maintenance products

400 N. 34th St., Ste. 202

Seattle, WA 98103

(800) 563-3057

www.nikwax.com

Tear-Aid

The best adhesive patches for repairing all things fabric

PO Box 1879

Land O Lakes, FL 34639

(800) 937-3716

www.tear-aid.com

ZRK Enterprises

Well-stocked zipper repair kits

279 Palm Ave.

Ashland, OR 97520

(541) 482-5020

www.zipperrescue.com

SERVICES

Most outdoor brands have excellent in-house repair and warranty departments and in many cases will make repairs for free or little cost. But when in doubt, call these fine folks. Rainy Pass Repair handles zipper problems, holes, tears, laundering, alterations, and just about any other fabric-related problem you could ever have.

Rainy Pass Repair

4415 Stone Way North

Seattle, WA 98103

(888) RIP-STOP (747-7867)

www.rainypass.com

Photo Credits

Page 89: Meg Erznoznik

Page 90: Steve Roy

Page 91: Meg Erznoznik

Page 93: Max Katzmartsic

Page 94: Meghan Kershner

Pages 95, 99: Kristin Hostetter

Page 100: Jonathan Dorn

Page 101: Steve Roy

Page 102: top, Kim Phillips; bottom, Max Katzmartsic

Page 103: Meg Erznoznik

Page 104: Kristin Hostetter

Page 106: Fullerton Images

Page 107: Steve Roy

Page 108: Kristin Hostetter

Page 110: Meg Erznoznik

Page 111: Steve Roy

Pages 112, 113: Katie Herrell

Page 114: top, Katie Herrell; bottom, licensed by Shutterstock.com

Page 115: Fullerton Images

Pages 116, 117: Kristin Hostetter

Page 118: Licensed by Shutterstock.com

Page 119: Meg Erznoznik

Page 120: Julia Vandenoever

Page 121: Meg Erznoznik

Page 122: top, Optimus; bottom, Meg Erznoznik

Page 123: Meg Erznoznik

Page 124: Genny Fullerton

Pages 125, 126, 127, 128, 129, 130: Meg Erznoznik

Page 132: top, Aaron Bellows; bottom, Meg Erznoznik

Page 133: Genny Fullerton

Page 134: Kristin Hostetter

Page 135: Licensed by Shutterstock.com

Pages 136, 138, 139: Meg Erznoznik

Page 140: Hydro-Photon Inc.

Page 141: Fullerton Images

Page 142: Meg Erznoznik

Page 143: Fullerton Images

Page 144: Steve Roy

Page 145: Kristin Hostetter

Page 146: Sarah Burnett

Pages 147, 148: Jennifer Howe / howephoto.us

Page 149: top, Matt Allouf; bottom, Steve Roy

Page 150: Meg Erznoznik

Page 151: top, Jennifer Howe / howephoto.us; bottom, Michael Urli

Page 152: Meg Erznoznik

Page 153: Jennifer Howe / howephoto.us

Page 154: Ryan Morrison

Page 156: Fullerton Images

Page 157: © Huguette Roe / Shutterstock.com

Page 158: Kristin Hostetter

Page 159: Meg Erznoznik

Page 161: Genny Fullerton

Page 162: Fullerton Images

Pages 163, 164, 165, 166, 167, 168, 169: Jennifer Howe / howephoto.us

Pages 170, 171: Genny Fullerton

Page 172: Julia Vandenoever

Page 173: Steve Roy

Page 174: Kim Phillips

Pages 175, 177: Kristin Hostetter

Page 180: Fullerton Images

Page 181: Kristin Hostetter

Page 182: Tim Murphy

Page 183: Mike Nancarrow

Pages 184, 185: Jennifer Howe / howephoto.us

Page 200: Tracy Ross

Index

About the Author

Kristin has been BACKPACKER magazine's gear editor since 1994. She has put thousands of camping and hiking products through BACKPACKER's rigorous gear-testing program. Her travels have taken her all over the world—from Alaska to Iceland, from Wales to Wyoming—in search of the best testing conditions, which often means the worst weather! She has appeared as a gear expert on NBC's *Today,* CBS's *The Early Show,* and *The Martha Stewart Show,* among others. Kristin is the author of three other books: *Don't Forget the Duct Tape, Adventure Journal,* and *Tent and Car Camper's Handbook.* Kristin is also known as the "Gear Pro" on backpacker.com, where she answers questions from readers about all sorts of outdoor skills and gear. She lives in Massachusetts with her husband and two sons, all of whom love to join Kristin on her adventures whenever possible.